The ABC'S of Distilling

The Ultimate Guide to Making Your Own Vodka, Whiskey, Rum, Brandy, Moonshine, and More

Steve O'Connor

© **Copyright 2018 Natalia Crimson - All rights reserved.**

The content contained within this book may not be reproduced, duplicated or transmitted without direct written permission from the author or the publisher.

Under no circumstances will any blame or legal responsibility be held against the publisher, or author, for any damages, reparation, or monetary loss due to the information contained within this book, either directly or indirectly.

Legal Notice:

This book is copyright protected. It is only for personal use. You cannot amend, distribute, sell, use, quote or paraphrase any part, or the content within this book, without the consent of the author or publisher.

Disclaimer Notice:

Please note the information contained within this document is for educational and entertainment purposes only. All effort has been executed to present accurate, up to date, reliable, complete information. No warranties of any kind are declared or implied. Readers acknowledge that the author is not engaged in the rendering of legal, financial, medical or professional advice.

The content within this book has been derived from various sources. Please consult a licensed professional before attempting any techniques outlined in this book.

By reading this document, the reader agrees that under no circumstances is the author responsible for any losses, direct or indirect, that are incurred as a result of the use of the information contained within this document, including, but not limited to, errors, omissions, or inaccuracies.

Table of Contents

Introduction 6

- **Chapter 1** 9
  What is distillation, and how is it done at home?

- **Chapter 2** 18
  Types of distilling methods

- **Chapter 3** 27
  Distilling equipment

- **Chapter 4** 37
  All about Yeast

- **Chapter 5** 49
  The process of fermentation

- **Chapter 6** 60
  What is alcohol filtration?

- ❖ **Chapter 7**..65

  Bottling and storage

- ❖ **Chapter 8**..76

  The most common problems and solutions

- ❖ **Chapter 9**..85

  Frequently asked questions

- ❖ **Chapter 10**..98

  How to create home-made whiskey

- ❖ **Chapter 11**..109

  How to make Brandy

- ❖ **Chapter 12**..121

  Creating moonshine

- ❖ **Chapter 13** 130

  How to make rum

❖ **Chapter 14**..140
   How to make vodka

❖ **Chapter 15**..153
   Mixing up for a beer

❖ **Chapter 16**..164
   How to create distilled wine

❖ **Chapter 17**..172
   Cleaning

Conclusion..174

Introduction

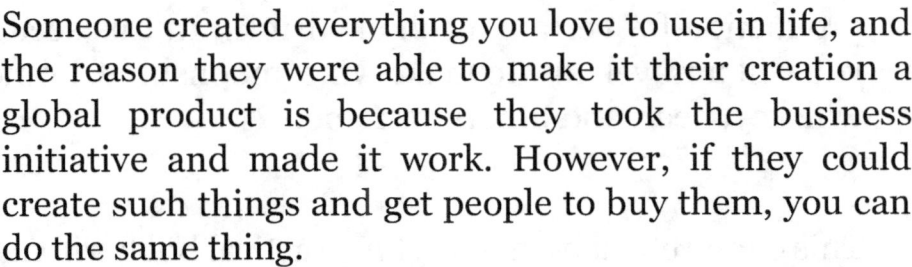

Someone created everything you love to use in life, and the reason they were able to make it their creation a global product is because they took the business initiative and made it work. However, if they could create such things and get people to buy them, you can do the same thing.

I believe that a significant reason why you are reading this book is that you love wine, brandy, whiskey, rum, and other forms of alcoholic beverage. Even if you like just one of them, the fact that you enjoy taking an occasional sip means you can commit to the process of learning how to make yours.

Distillation at home is possible, and it is one of the best ways of getting your unique blend and brand of your preferred alcoholic beverage. This material will introduce you to the concept of distillation at home.

This book is divided into two parts. The first part introduces you to the fundamental ideas of distillation at home, which includes the different methods, required equipment, the fermentation process, storage, and bottling. This first part will empower you with information on what you should do, how to do it, and the kind of tools you will need to make it happen.

You will also gain insight into some common distillation problems and the most practical solutions.

Part two is where we get to work as it is a practical section that entails you learning the specifics of production for certain alcoholic drinks. In this section, you will unravel how to make wine, moonshine, brandy, whiskey, beer, and others at home.

This comprehensive and highly practical book will make it easier for you to create your unique mixture of ingredients that will stand out from the ones bought at the store. But before we embark on our journey, you should know that distillation at home is illegal in some states or countries.

As such, before you start the process of distillation at home, please make sure you are not breaking any laws. Yes, I want to impart you with knowledge and information, but I also want you to do things the right way. More so, you can still hold on to the information received through this material, even if you have such restrictive policies in your state. But only practice and use them when you are sure that you are not breaking the law.

We are ready to dive into the process as we begin our exploration with the foundational aspects of distillation

This first part is akin to the theoretical aspect of the lessons you learn in school. Here you will unravel foundational ideas that will largely influence the practical section of this book.

At this stage, you are not required to practice anything, just read and learn.

When you get to part two, the significance of what you read in this chapter will be glaring and useful. But pay attention to every detail that will be shared below as it will enable you to take the right steps at the practical section.

Chapter One

What is distillation, and how is it done at home?

We will begin our exploration with the fundamental and foundational idea of distilling at home and how the process is achieved.

This first chapter gives a general overview of what you should know about distillation at home. There will be more information in subsequent sections, and you will surely gain additional insight into the theoretical and practical nature of the process.

But first, you have been introduced to the idea, and I want you to have a solid foundation on the concept before we move on to other aspects.

Some people think that the idea of making beer only entails getting some potato, cooking it and BOOM! Your beer is ready!

Is this entirely true?

Well, you will need potato for some recipes, but it isn't solely about boiling it and getting the beer. There are other aspects to consider and more specific details you must become conversant with which is why we are embarking on this detailed journey together.

The first idea you should know is that distilling at home is still mostly illegal in some countries.

In some other countries, it is not prohibited, but in some, it is restricted as such even though you are learning something amazing, you must become conscious of what the law says about the topic. If you must go ahead with it, then you must do it within the ambits of the law.

After understanding the law of your state or city regarding home distillation, you can move on to knowing the meaning of the fundamental concept: distillation.

Distillation refers to the process of mixing two or more liquids or starchy material to be brewed into liquor. When an alcoholic beverage is distilled, it means it is obtained from wine or some other fermented fruit juice.

Some famous examples of distilled liquor include brands such as whisky, gin, rum, arrack etc.

In this material, you will learn how to distil alcohol at home without the complex processes of a mass production done in distilling companies.

In addition to learning how to distil, you will also discover how to create your unique blends of alcoholic beverages.

Regardless of the recipe you use, you will need to purchase a still, which is one of the most consistent tools with the distillation process. The still is also known as a heat source that boils the fermented liquid to a steam level (since alcohol has a low boiling point than water) with cold water loop that creates a chilly surface area inside so the steam condenses and collects your final product.

You will also need a lot of other materials that will help you through the process. All the materials you will need will be discussed in detail in chapter three, where we consider distillation tools.

But before we get there, some of these tools include big plastic tubs, stockpots, carboys etc. Unlike some other homemade processes where the tools and ingredients are not easily purchased the ones for home, distillation can be bought in most stores (online and offline).

There is an array of spirits and wine you can distil at home, but if you are a beginner, I will recommend that you start with something that is already fermented (you will find the recipe for distilled wine in chapter sixteen).

Starting with wine that is already fermented gives you an opportunity to learn how to use the still before you go through the fermentation process.

After all, you wouldn't want to dedicate so much time to creating the right fermentation and end up failing at the distillation point.

It is okay to start with store-bought wine as an excellent way to begin your learning experience with distilling at home.

When you start distilling your mash or your wash you can start with the basic ideas of using sugar (when you get to section two which is the practical section, these concepts about sugar will make a lot of sense to you so don't worry).

So you can start with sugar, or you can use grains to add some flavor into your mash.

You should know that with grains, you have to be much more finicky with the process, but it is always worth it in the end. Most of the steps you will take with home distillation are the same with only slight variations, so if you get it right with one recipe, there is a huge chance of you getting it right with another one.

To source for equipment and ingredients, you may have to look around shops that stock the items you need. For most of the edible ingredients such as grains and fruits, you can get fresh ones at your local farmers market or grocery stores. Yeast is also another crucial ingredient you will need, and it has to be excellent yeast (you will learn more about yeast in chapter four).

As for the stills they come in a variety of styles, but as a beginner, you may want to keep it simple by sticking with the traditional types of stills. If you have a stockpot meant for mashing and a big plastic bucket for the fermentation process, you will be halfway through with your tools. A still is the last tool you and it is a closed pot with a tube out at the top along with a heat source.

Due to the possibility of an explosion, while working with stills, you have to be very careful with this tool.

Explosions while brewing at home is one of the reasons why distilling alcohol at home is still illegal in some countries. With stills, you have to also pay attention to the content it produces.

More so explosions happen when a person distils in an enclosed space, and this makes it easier for the alcohol fumes to build up.

When the alcohol builds up to such high levels, the potential for explosion increases. Explosions also happen when the system releases pure ethanol which can lead to flames.

Working with stills also means that the liquid will make contact with the condenser, which also means there is a high potential for lead- poisoning. However, lead-poisoning only happens when you use the wrong metal; hence the reason copper coils are the best.

The first part of the liquid that comes out is not drinkable, and there is a way to tell the parts that are consumable (you will learn more about this in the practical section). The entire liquid you distil is not always delicious; the first part will probably taste like nail polish (this is the heads). The second last part known as tails is a wrong beer, and you must discard it.

Another prominent concept with distilling at home is the idea of ageing the wine. Most people do not age small scale wine production like the one done at home, but if you love to have a distinct blend, you might want to consider ageing.

Oak chips added to the mixture in the barrel are tremendous and if you're going to age your wine, then use barrels (bottles are not ideal).

Barrels contribute immensely to the colour, richness and uniqueness of the flavour you create with your wine. If you create whisky, then charred oak barrels are suitable for the ageing process. There are also variants of barrels for other specific kinds of wine you create.

To create the perfect alcoholic blend at home, you must become a person who pays close attention to details, especially details about temperature.

The success of your home distillation process is largely hinged on how well you watch the temperature while the wash heats up. If the temperature is excessively high, you will get a different kind of product, and if it is too low, the same thing will happen. If you neglect the temperature, the concentration of alcohol will be higher, and this is known as "Fusel alcohols" or "Fusel oils" (it looks oily).

 If you have this fusel flavour in your distilled spirit, when it is consumed, you will have a nasty hangover, feel nauseous, vomit, headaches and even acute illness.

Mostly if you are unsure of the temperature when you distil the first time, you can gain certainty by taking on a second distillation process which should be done slowly. With the second distillation take care to monitor the temperature.

Distilling at home helps you become more conversant with the process of creating something unique that suits your particular taste buds. But the process itself is like learning a new skill which means you have to be patient during preparation. At first, everything may seem strange, but after your first trial and subsequent ones, you will become familiar with the concept.

There are numerous things to consider with this process, and there are a lot of things to note, which will affect the result you get. Most people who give up on this idea do not take the time to learn the basic concept first, but this wouldn't be your case because this book offers a balanced narrative.

Think about when you were in a classroom or learnt something new, did you get right to the evaluation process?

Or did you study the course content first?

Of course, you had to research first before application, you have learned the basic ideas with this chapter, and it is time to build on the information with subsequent sections.

So the risk of you making huge mistakes is mainly minimized because you have received proper teachings on the idea.

There are some peculiar things you must note about the distilling method because it is at the core of the liquor production process.

Head over to the next chapter to learn more about distilling methods.

Chapter Two

Types of distilling methods

Although you will be distilling on a small scale level at home, you must know the significant kinds of distilling techniques. Distilling is an aspect of wine/spirit production that remains constant even when recipes change (you must distil).

So in this chapter, you will learn more about the techniques.

If you visit a modern distillery, you will find very tall columns that are connected by a network of tubes. You will also find squat pots and pumps that aid the production of some of your favourite wine. Distillation is mostly related to the ancient process of alchemy, but it is also simpler than alchemy: the basic idea for distillation is creating alcohol from a lower base.

So one may wonder "Why can' winemakers ferment their mixtures to a higher level instead of distilling?"

Well, the answer lies within the use of yeast in the process. When yeast eats up the sugar (which happens to make beer, spirits, wine, etc.), it creates alcohol, CO_2 and other waste products. However, if more alcohol and CO_2 is created, there will be less sugar for the yeast, and at some point, the alcohol will become too toxic for the yeast.

For us to strike a balance with this process and to get a high ABV level, we must separate the alcohol from water through evaporation and the process of condensation (which is the essence of distillation). Due to its lower boiling point than water (alcohol), the winemakers can evaporate the alcohol, collect vapour into the tube and with cold temperature force the alcohol to condense into a liquid.

Methods of distillation

There are generally two methods of distillation, and other forms originate from these two:

The Alembic method

(which is also known as the pit distilling method)

The alembic method is one of the oldest means of distillation (It was first used in alchemy).

Alembic is a big vessel (like the shape of a kettle), and the wash is heated inside.

While heating up ethanol evaporates before the water, the liquid then travels into a cooling tube and into another vessel to condense.

With less water present the ABV will be higher, but aside from the ethanol there will also be other compounds such as methanol, tannis etc. these compounds also have to evaporate during distillation because their continuous presence in the liquid will affect the flavor. Distillation is meant to ensure that the winemaker gets the right amount of alcohol and all flavoring compounds into the finished product.

The column distilling method

This method became famous as a result of the success of the pot distilling method. As we advanced into the modern world, a lot of commercial distillers started to seek out very easy and faster means of distilling their products. With the alembic method, they had to wash the pot stills after each batch of wine which was time-consuming.

So the column distilling technique is a solution to that problem as it entails the use of giant columns. With this technique, the mash is injected into the column, and the steam can be easily set at the right temperature.

All undesired compounds are left behind, and this method also doesn't require much cleaning like the first one. Repeated distillation processes are possible with this technique, and it is mostly used by commercial brewers who make large batches of wine.

In addition to these top two distillation techniques, there are other forms of distillation that draw inspiration from these two or use their tools and processes to achieve results.

Some of them include:

Fractional distillation

With fractional distillation, alcohol is repeatedly purified to remove water and unwanted elements. Typically, a fermentation mix contains water and ethyl alcohol with a small amount of compounds that make up the flavour of the final product.

The stills used in the fractional distillation process have a multi- column rectifying system that will release pure distillate (with a minimal amount of unwanted elements).

To understand this technique well enough, we have to juxtapose it with the simple distillation technique so you can understand how it differs from it and what makes this method unique.

This technique is a modified version of the simple distillation process which separates complex solutions into varying compounds through their different boiling points.

With the simple distillation method, the distillate you get will have a higher level of alcoholic concentration, but water will still be in the mix.

So what you can do is to re-distil to gain a higher alcoholic concentration level. What fractional distillation does is to improve on this simple method by performing the multiple distillations once. The distillation can happen once because of the kind of column used, which is crafted based on how the process occurs.

Another distinction between this process and the simple one is that with simple distillation the vapours from the boiling liquid rises to a column and as the temperature at the height of the column decreases the elements in the mixture will be less volatile.

Then condensation takes place in another column (the columns re few centimeters apart).

The second distillation happens with the simple method as the vapors rise and bubble up to the condenser plates. The vapors are then cleaned and purified, but with the fractional distillation, method winemakers can achieve both processes at the same time.

Continuous distillation

This kind of distillation process aims at ensuring continuous operations with winemaking.

The liquid is fed into a still column (it is inspired by the column method) and an equal amount of liquid consistently exists as the mixture distillates. With continuous distillation, professional distillers will not have to empty the still and reload it every time they want a new batch which means it is a more efficient distillation process.

Continuous distillation is also a continuous process with which distillates can flow at a high output level. While this is going on the raw materials for making the wine can be fed into the still at some point without interrupting the collection of finished products.

With the older forms of distillation, the still must be emptied to reload, and this makes the distillation process tiring. The fact that this process is uninterrupted makes it one of the ideal options for distillation.

Although as a beginner and homemade winemaker, you may not have to use this process just yet.

Steam distillation

The steam distillation technique distils alcohol by passing steam gotten from the pot still through plant material. This method is easily controlled, and it is a distillation process that gives the assurance of better quality alcohol as a finished product. The process entails the placement of fresh botanical material in the plant inside the still, and then it is pressurized.

While under pressure, the steam is generated in another chamber in the still and passes through the organic material to remove all oils.

As the steam passes the organic material, the essential compounds of the mixture will be released.

The distillate that contains a mix of water vapour and other elements will return to its liquid form after its condensed.

This steam technique is the same process as the simple distillation method as the slight difference between both ideas is the use of steam. When you sue steam distillation for alcohol, you will be retaining the delicate flavours, essence and aromas of the mixture that would have been broken down if it is exposed to a higher temperature.

The steam distillation process is the most preferred method used in the production of Gin because it aids the retention of flavours from aromatic plants. Alcohol can also be made from fermented properties that are placed on the column of the alembic still (a good example is leftover pressed grape skins).

Regardless of how you are distilling your alcohol always remember that alcohol never evaporates alone. Other compounds such as fusel alcohols, methanol and esters can evaporate with it. The idea of "Cutting" is the term used to describe the separation of these other elements through temperature and proper timing.

For example, methanol evaporates at 148.5F, so a winemaker can assert that any liquid that shows up before 173 F should be thrown out. With this example, you can understand that precision is crucial for all distillers because it enables you to focus on the tiniest details that make a difference with the final product.

Distillation has to be done right at all times for you to get the perfect blend and the techniques are crucial.

In this chapter, you discovered some of the essential distillation techniques. Now you understanding of the subject matter has increased but we still have to build on the information you've received.

We are still building on the foundational and theoretical aspect of the book, so in the next chapter, we will focus more on distilling equipment and what you will purchase while preparing for your winemaking process.

Chapter Three

Distilling equipment

When you decide to learn something new, especially something you have to create, it is vital that you know the types of equipment and tools you will need.

Of course, it is possible that from what you have read thus far you already have an idea as to what you will need but do you know them specifically?

So in this chapter, you will uncover a comprehensive list of all distilling equipment needed to help you create a great-tasting bottle(s) of wine. Most of the items you will find in this chapter are easily accessible as you can purchase them online or at physical stores.

More so, before making a purchase, it is advised that you make sure all tools are in good condition.

Temperature gauge (thermometer)

A thermometer gauges the temperature of your setup, and it is very crucial equipment. You determine the temperature with this tool by placing it at the top of the column during distillation.

Also, you can have a thermometer inside the pot still to monitor the distilling activity happening inside the container.

The thermometer should be affixed to the still, so its sensors are protected from pressure. The most flexible type of thermometer is the handheld one which comes in both Celsius and Fahrenheit gauges (hence you wouldn't have to convert). You can get thermometers are hardware stores.

A hydrometer

This tool measures the gravity, sugar content and alcoholic content of your solution. This equipment is a small float that can either sink or float based on the density of the liquid. If it drops deeper, it means there is a higher concentration of alcohol. The hydrometer can also ascertain when fermentation ends.

Siphon

The purpose of the siphon is to get the main content of your mixture out while leaving the sediments behind. To achieve the right siphoning process, you must use suitable equipment as there are several siphoning tools out there.

Some winemakers struggle with siphoning because even when they use a siphon, they end up stirring up the sediments again.

So here are some of the best kind of siphons:

Auto siphon

You can start the siphoning process without any movement using this tool. This equipment has both the features of a racking cane and pump; all you have to do is attach it to the siphon hose and slowly slide the tube inside slowly to start siphoning.

Racking canes

Racking cane is a rigid tube that makes it easier for winemakers to point to where they want to draw from. This equipment can be attached to the end of the siphon hose (just like a wand). At the bottom of the tube, you will find a diversion tip which ensures you don't draw from the bottom of the container (this is where the sediments have settled).

Racking tube clamps

To ensure that you disturb or stir up the deposits, you can use the racking tube clamps. This tool acts as a third party that keeps everything secure and in one position without moving.

Airlock

You will need the airlock during fermentation as it allows the carbon dioxide released during fermentation to escape the fermenter while avoiding oxidation.

You can either purchase an airlock from a hardware store or make one yourself.

Heat source

Heat is needed during wine production as you are supposed to heat your kettle. You can use a gas burner, electric controller or an electric hot plate. Most of these heat sources are affordable, and if you don't want to buy a new one, you can use what you have at home just ensure that it is suitable for the still.

A spirit hydrometer

If you are distilling whisky, then you will need this equipment to determine the final alcohol percentage by volume (ABV). With this equipment, you can distil the finest whisky as it helps you strike a balance with your ingredients and final product.

Stainless steel spoon

A stainless steel spoon is one of the most essential yet straightforward equipment required for the process. This tool enables you to mix the ingredients thoroughly and aids de-gassing (the process of removing suspended carbon dioxide left over from fermentation).

Still

There are two major categories of stills: the pot still and the reflux still.

Most of the stills you see today are either a form of these two or a hybrid. Pot stills are the simplest types, and it is popular with distillers.

Pot stills are great for spirits with base flavour because it allows the ingredients to flow over the distillate. The reflux stills are not as simple as the pot stills, but they are great in helping winemakers avoid a second distillation run.

Cleaners/sanitizers

Keeping your wine free from contamination starts even before you take the first step so you must get sanitizers and cleaning tools that will help you keep all equipment neat.

Bottles and corks

You will also need wine bottles and corks as this will be the holding containers for your finished product. To know more about bottling and storage head over to chapter seven for comprehensive details.

Acid test kit

This kit will help you test wine samples for acid level so you can tell if you need to make adjustments or not.

If your wine is too acidic, it will have a sharp, unpleasant taste, and if it is too low in acid, the taste will be stale. Now if your recipe is spot- on with clear directions, you may not have problems with acidity levels, but you can also get the acid test kit in case of an emergency

A crusher

You will need a crusher if you are using fruits as the base for your wine. A good fruit crusher will make it easier for you to start the process of creating your homemade wine.

Nylon mesh straining bag

A nylon bag is a need for your mash, and it will be beneficial if you got a large bag that can hold more of the ingredient you will use for the mash.

Large and small digital scales

The large digital scale will be to measure the grains and other ingredients you will need for the base of your alcohol. The small digital scale is to measure the yeast (you have to get it right with yeast measurement).

This book seeks to empower you with information on how to create different alcoholic drinks as such the tools needed for each recipe may have slight variations. Overall the equipment mentioned above will help you get the job done (regardless of the recipe you use).

However, there are specific ideas regarding distilling equipment for unique recipes, and we will round off this section by discussing such peculiarities:

Firstly if you are making rum, you will need fewer materials than some other methods. You will only need essential items like the fermenting bucket, airlock (which is optional), carboy and yeast. As you create the rum, you can use other tools to determine temperature, pH etc.

If you are making brandy, then you will need fruit juice and yeast (this is the base of the wine). Also, carboy and airlock are required tools. To mash the fruit, you will also need a crusher, but again brandy requires less effort than rum.

With whisky, the method of production you use will determine the kind of equipment to use. For example, if you use the extraction method, you will only have to mix the extract, yeast and water in a carboy (that's all!).

If you are using the grain method, you will need more equipment which includes a grain mill (this is helpful only if you are not using the pre-crushed grains). You will also need a mash tun that is used for preparing the mash, fermentation bucket and hot liquor tank.

For vodka and other neutral wines they can be made from sugar base or grains. Sugar base method is more straightforward, thus requires less equipment, the grain method is also similar, and potato vodka is the same.

You have been reading about distillation from chapter one because it is a core aspect of the alcohol making process (it is also our subject matter).

With this first three chapters, you now understand the meaning of distillation, the distillation techniques as well as required equipment.

So it is safe to say we have done well with the distillation aspect of our discourse.

It is time to build on all that information with a section on an essential ingredient you will need for homemade wine/spirits.

Can you guess the name?

Head over to chapter four to learn all about YEAST!

*You will find most of this equipment in the second section when we start practising with wine recipes.

Chapter Four

All about Yeast

What is an essential ingredient needed to make a delicious beef burger?

The answer is beef!

Without beef, in the burger, it cannot be called a "Beefburger".

Yeast is to alcohol the same way meat is to beef burger! The yeast added to the mixture while making your unique blend of a drink is one of the most important ingredients because its reaction to sugar is what produces the alcohol.

This chapter will be all about yeast, as you will learn how it contributes to your final product. A lot of mistakes winemakers at home make is attributed to struggles with yeast.

For some of these brewers, they seek to understand how yeast works so they can perfect the recipes they use.

Yeast is a single-celled microorganism reproduced through budding, and they are classified as "Fungi". Yeast is also responsible for converting fermentable sugar to alcohol (and some other by- products). There are numerous varieties of yeasts, and in past times there were only two types of beer yeast known as ale yeast and lager yeast.

Yeast is what distinguishes wine from an average grape juice as in the absence of alcohol; yeast converts to sugar, and in wine grapes, it transforms into alcohol and carbon dioxide through the fermentation process.

If the grapes have more sugars, then the alcohol level will be very high, which is why some winemakers stop fermentation early so they can reduce the alcohol production from yeast interacting with sugar.

Winemakers also stop the fermentation process early because they want some sweetness left in the wine (this mostly applies to dessert wines). When the fermentation temperature is reduced, the yeast will become inactive; the mixture will be filtered, thus killing the yeast cells.

Although there are many types of yeast for the winemaking process, the most common one is known as Saccharomyces Cerevisiae. This kind of yeast is mostly used because of several factors.

Firstly, saccharomyces cerevisiae has a predictable fermentation capacity which means that after using it for a while, you can get used to it and know when it becomes active.

This yeast is also a top choice for brewers because of its ability to thrive in wine pH levels and its relatively high alcoholic tolerance.

Yeast successfully converts sugar to alcohol through a metabolic process that requires the presence of oxygen-producing energy for the cell. Through fermentation with yeast, ethanol is also produced as a waste product in the wine, and if the yeast cells remain healthy, fermentation will be complete.

In addition to turning sugar to alcohol, yeast also produces other compounds in the winemaking process.

Yeast produces methanol which is found in minimal amounts in red wine.

Fusel oils are also produced by yeast through the decomposition of amino acids. Succinic acid is also produced by yeast at the earliest stage of fermentation, and acetic acid (a volatile acid) is formed through yeast strains.

There are factors to consider when selecting yeasts for your wine, and there are good reasons why you should settle for the right yeast as well.

Firstly, the different yeasts available for use produce varying flavours and aroma in the finished wine. The different flavour is due to how the yeast digests sugar and nutrients.

Secondly, the choice of yeast is crucial because not all strains have the

same level of alcohol tolerance. While some wild yeasts have tolerance of up to 5-6%, some others can have up to 18% and even more.

So how can you choose the right yeast?

What are the factors to consider when selecting yeast?

Let's find the answers!

How to select winemaking yeast

Step one

Choose your flavour profile

First, you have to consider the flavour you will like to create. For example, some fungi are not great for specific drinks while they are perfect for others. So if you use the right yeast for the wrong drink, you will surely have issues and vice versa.

Also, some yeasts are supposed to be used without any other addition or strains. You can tell more about the yeast by reading labels and adhering to the manufacturer's instructions. Some yeasts do not pack a lot of flavours or aromas while some others have to be paired with another strain to get the right results.

Let your choice of wine flavour be the determining factor with this yeast selection process.

Step two

Check yeast alcohol tolerance

Next, you have to ascertain the alcohol tolerance of the yeast (this is where you ensure that the yeast can ferment your wine). Read labels of yeast and do a test run of the product first using smaller batches of your winemaking process.

If the yeast is not good, it will not finish fermenting, and it will be sweeter than you would have preferred.

Step three

Estimate alcohol content

To estimate the alcohol content, you have to take a gravity reading. Make sure you use the correct gravity temperature so you can get an accurate reading.

To calculate this, you should assume that your wine will finish at 0.990 gravity (yes this is low, but it is possible).

Then measure the specific gravity and estimated final gravity with the equation below:

%ABV = (original SG − Final SG)/7.36 * 1000

Use this formula for yeast alcoholic tolerance to see if it will ferment well. You will need a hydrometer for this.

Step four

Check expiration date and duration

Even if you get an excellent yeast that meets all the criteria, if it has stayed for too long on the shelf or if it is expired, it will be useless to you.

So don't be in a burry when you are searching for good yeast, take your time to get one that is still active and fresh.

If you use an old or expired yeast, it will affect the flavour, aroma and taste of your finished product.

In some cases, the wine wouldn't ferment properly when the yeast is not good enough, which means all your efforts will come to nothing.

Step five

Speak with an expert (if you have to)

Lastly, some experienced brewers have used a lot of yeasts variants in the past. If you are still unsure about the yeast to use, please ask someone who is a brewing expert for guidance. You will be amazed at the yeast options you get, which will also help you narrow down your selection.

A right way of getting over the entire yeast selection process is relying on information from those who have worked with yeast repeatedly.

Also, feel free to experiment so you can find the perfect type for your winemaking process.

Step six

Nutrient requirement

The nutrient requirement is a crucial factor because the yeast will face adverse fermentation processes. An example of adverse fermentation processes includes high sugar which happens when the grapes you use are deficient in nutrients.

Poorly cultivated grapes will be deficient in yeast nutrient as some yeast strains will have higher nutrients that will ferment faster than others. So what you should do is ensure that you have the nutrients that can boost your yeast cells if the grapes or fruits you use are not top quality.

Nitrogen is an example of an essential nutrient that can boost yeast cell growth. Such nutrients can help the yeast survive, multiple well enough and ferment successfully. This step also reemphasizes the importance of planning when preparing to make wine because the plan will help you chose a yeast strain that suits your choice of wine in every way.

Before you start the process of making your wine investigate the fruits, you will use (especially if fruits are involved). Get to know the farming and environmental conditions of the fruit as well as physical deformities such as rot which is a sign that the fruit is not good enough.

If you already have the grapes with mild rot on them and you have no other choice but to use it, then you will need yeast with additional nutrients to make up for the deficiency.

If it is a colouring challenge, you will have to get a yeast strain that enables colour extraction. So you can see that there is a connection between yeast and other ingredients which is why all winemakers must gain knowledge on how to use yeast.

In some cases, the yeast is not strong enough to finish the fermentation process well if this happens to you there are two options you can take. The first option is for you to select another yeast with the kind of tolerance level you seek.

But if you are already at the fermentation stage, this option might not help you so you can pitch the yeast as it is and find a strain strong enough for the content you have.

Which means that the first yeast used will do the more significant part of the fermenting process (providing flavour and aroma) and the second yeast will have its minimal impact as well (after all you just want to complete the fermentation process).

Even when your choice of yeast strain is excellent for your wine, if the fermentation environment is not right, it will not be activated. The fermentation environment plays a very crucial role, which is why getting the right yeast is not enough; you've got to pay attention to other factors as well.

Some of the factors you should observe include how the amount of nutrient and oxygen affects the fermentation process because the yeast has to be happy. All the elements and considerations thus far were mentioned with the assumption that your environment and conditions for wine production are perfect.

More importantly, make sure you have the yeast ready before the production day. If you decide to wait until the exact day, you will start production; you might not have the time to implement all the ideas shared thus far in this chapter.

Most of the ideas shared here are activities, things to do and observations to make before the day of production.

Just like the beef burger if you get things right with your yeast selection process while making your wines/spirits, you will have a great tasting final product. Too many beginners fail to pay close attention to the yeast they use, and this is the start of problems for them.

With this chapter, you have gained insight into the nature of yeasts and how you can maximize its value for your winemaking process. Remember to always stick to good yeast because it makes a whole lot of difference while preparing your homemade wine.

Fermentation is also a necessary process that is made possible because of yeast which is why we will be considering all about it in the next chapter.

What is fermentation, and what are the factors to consider when fermenting your wine?

Read on to get answers and more.

Chapter Five

The process of fermentation

Having a good knowledge of the fermentation process is very important because this is what helps you with the winemaking procedure.

Now if you have a detailed and perfect recipe, you may not need extra information on how to ferment, but it is always advisable that you know how to works so you can get it right at all times.

Wine fermentation happens when the yeast consumes sugar and converts it to half alcohol and half CO_2 gas (which is the process of carbonation).

So for example, if you have 5 gallons of juice with 10 pounds of sugar inside, you will ferment the sugar with yeast and have about 5 pounds of alcohol.

The remaining 5 pounds of sugar will become CO_2 so that the batch will be 5 pounds lighter.

The fermentation process also happens in two stages:

1. The primary fermentation stage (sometimes called aerobic fermentation)

2. The secondary fermentation stage (also known as anaerobic fermentation)

The primary fermentation

This type of fermentation last for the 3-5 days and 70% of the fermentation activity happens in these first days. In some cases, you will observe foaming during the time of increasing fermentation.

This primary fermentation is also known as aerobic fermentation because the vessel used for the process is allowed to remain open.

The air that goes into the vessel helps multiple the yeast. Alcohol will be produced during fermentation, but a more significant part of the yeast will also reproduce itself.

The Secondary fermentation

This process happens when the remaining 30% of fermentation activity happens.

Unlike the primary process where fermentation happens within five days, fermentation with this approach lasts for about two weeks (based on the amount of sugar and nutrient available in the mix).

Secondary fermentation takes more time as it has less activity with each day that passes. You can also attach an airlock to the vessel at this time to reduce the inflow of air.

This reduction in airflow makes the yeast forget about multiplication and gives energy to making alcohol.

However, you should know that secondary fermentation is NOT a second fermentation process (this term is usually confusing for a lot of people).

Second fermentation happens when the excess sugar that wasn't consumed by the yeast restarts fermentation.

This situation occurs when a wine is sweetened again before all the yeast is used up.

Sometimes second fermentation happens by accident except for sparkling wines. Sparkling wines are meant to be bottled before the yeast loses flavour.

But aside from the types of fermentation processes, you should also know some important considerations that make the process successful.

Temperature

Temperature plays a crucial role in fermentation because if it is too cold, the yeast will not enable fermentation quickly, and this makes the yeast dormant. If the temperature is too warm, the yeast will ferment just fine, but the flavour will be negatively affected.

The best kind of temperature for fermentation is 72 degrees (you can also use between 70-75 degrees).

Transferring the wine

As the wine ferments, you will have to move it off the sediment to a clean container (this is the process known as racking).

The transfer should be done at the end of primary fermentation or when the reading on your hydrometer shows 1.030.

The racking should also be done after the secondary fermentation process before boiling the wine.

Clearing

After the fermentation activity ends, you have to give it time to become bright enough for bottling. The yeast can take up to 2-4 weeks to clear up after fermentation completes.

Yeats expiration date

If your yeast is too old, the wine will not ferment properly, and this means you will have to start all over again. To prevent such a situation, you must always ensure that your yeast is as good as it should be for the process of fermentation.

Good yeast during this process is essential, but some people fail to get it right; hence the reason they are unhappy with their final alcoholic product.

Now you may be wondering when you can tell that your wine fermentation process is complete. Well, there are some clues you can use to determine when fermentation is over.

The first clue is a visible one which is the appearance of bubbles rising from the bottom to the top (just as it is with carbonated drinks).

If the wine is fermenting, you will also see bits of fruits pulp flowing about in the wine. Also, pay attention to the wine's edges you will also spot bubbles.

If you are working with an airlock, then bubbles through the airlock is a good sign that pressure in the vessel is higher (which means fermentation is happening). But you should know that bubbles appearing on the airlock also has a different interpretation as it also informs you when fermentation is not complete.

When wine is still fermenting, it is mostly not clear as some wines remain cloudy during fermentation. After fermentation, you may get a more transparent product, and this is when you know you are ready for the next phase.

You can tell that fermentation is complete through a gravity measurement (you can do this with a hydrometer or a refractometer).

Take the readings are intervals and ensure that all the readings show similar values.

Don't hurry to get the wine into bottles because you might age it. So take your time when fermenting because it can go on for days.

But when you leave it to ferment for days, it doesn't mean you should leave it desolate and untouched. You've to stir it at least once or twice in a day so you can prevent the pulps from being too dry while the wine ferments.

If you are using a standard fermentation bag, open it and stir but if you are using a more substantial bag, leave it open and give the pulp a quick stir.

If you don't occasionally stir like this, the pulp will become too dry, and this will give way for moulds of bacteria to grow in the wine.

Also, you have to stir is to prevent a dry layer from forming as this can interrupt the fermentation process.

How to avoid problems during fermentation

• Your choice of yeast should be one with high temperature and alcoholic tolerance.

• Don't use improperly stored yeast.

• Make sure residues from pesticides on fruits are washed off thoroughly (you should ensure that all fruits used are free from pesticides)

• Follow the manufacturer's instructions with yeasts, always check the temperature and rehydrate the yeast correctly.

• Avoid using over-ripe fruits as well because they contain high amounts of sugar which also means they will produce a high level of alcoholic content. Now the problem is that yeast cannot multiply effectively in an environment with 16-18% of alcohol.

• You can also add nitrogen to the mix through diammonium phosphate (this nutrient will help feed the yeast)

•Also, avoid overdoing the mixture with sulphites (which could be sulphur dioxide solutions). If the levels of this compound are too high, the yeast will be unable to react adequately.

•Do not add vitamins during fermentation because when it is leftover in the mix, it can lead to microbes. You can add nutrients before the fermentation process starts or as you add the yeast

•Clean and sanitize all tools used during the fermentation process, especially when you are starting a new batch of production. The yeast will function well without the presence of bacteria, and you will have to deal with bacteria when you have unsterilized tools.

There is also the idea of a stopped ferment which refers to when the winemaker stops the fermentation process. The process could have been stopped because the winemaker wants the sweetness of the wine to balance its acidity.

It could also be stopped because the winemaker doesn't want it to have too much alcohol.

However, stopped ferment is not always successful mostly when you want more sugar in the wine. The yeast will naturally continue to consume sugar, so what you should do is get rid of the yeast cells first to stop fermentation completely. Which means you might have to add SO_2, but please be careful when doing this because if you put too much sulphur, it can lead to an overdose.

Some persons follow through with a recipe and still get an alcoholic drink that tastes like vinegar after fermentation.

Well, the reason for the vinegar issue could be because of the presence of acetic acid in the jar you used to collect your wine.

Acetic acid is what gives vinegar its taste, and if you pour your wine into a jar containing this substance, your wine will have that vinegar taste.

To eliminate the taste, you must ensure that all jars and containers to be used are properly washed to remove traces of the unwanted substance in your finished product.

If you can ferment adequately, you will have done the most critical aspect of the winemaking process.

When preparing your ingredients and using the instructions on your recipes, make sure you pay closer attention to the fermentation process because it is essential.

Once fermentation is over, you can say your wine is almost ready, but first, you have to filter the mixture.

Filtration helps you get rid of particles and solids that may remain in the content, and you will learn more about this process in the next part.

Chapter Six

What is alcohol filtration?

Fermentation is at the heart of the creation process, but there is one more important part known as filtration.

Filtration is always done towards the end of the winemaking process. Just before bottling your wine, remove all particles bacteria or yeast, so your wine is purified.

When wine is filtered correctly, it becomes healthier and cleaner and affects the ageing process positively. Think about creating a masterpiece alcoholic beverage and getting so excited about drinking it. Then while drinking, you chew on bits of ingredients that should have been filtered?

You will surely be disappointed, and such disappointment is what this chapter is trying to help you avoid.

Now there are three main wine filtration methods, and we will explore all of them:

1. The gravity flow
2. The pump filtration
3. The hand pump method

The gravity flow

This method is the cheapest method from all the approaches. This method works by connecting a filter body (that has a filter pad) with a siphon tube.

The tube pushes the wine through the filter, but it is one of the slowest ways to get your final product.

More so, in some instances, particles from the wine may get into the filter pads. This situation means you will have to buy more filtration pads to re-filter the final product. You can either get the coarse filter pads which add some polish to the wine without losing colour.

The polish/medium pads are also a prevalent option as well as the sterile pads, which removes a lot of particles and the effects of oxidation in the wine.

When you affix the filter pad to the tube ensure that you've got your barrel or collection container below. Then fasten the outtake siphon tube and make sure your bottle or barrel is well placed to avoid any leakage.

Open the release part of the tool as the wine starts flowing through it to the filter pad, down to your bottle. As you fill the containers, replace one with another, then observe the particles in the filter pad. If the particles are too much, remove the used one and replace it with another one.

When you are done filtering make sure you wash the filtration system with water and sulphite solution,

Remember always to sterilize your filtration system before use.

The pump filtration

With the pump system, two people are required to make it work, and this method is faster than the gravity filtration system. You have to connect the outtake siphon tube to an empty bottle then open the release on the barrel. While one person operates the pump, another person should steady the container on the bottle and switch the containers as well.

Always observe the particles as they build on the filter pad and change the pad as you go on. At this stage, you may have to purchase filtration powder and apply it to the wine in minimal doses. As you add the powder continue to use the filtration system (this is also known as the powder filtration system)

The hand pump method

For this method, you will have to buy a powered pump filtration system which is the fastest of all three methods. It is also the most expensive and it works by either creating a vacuum which pulls the wine through a filter or through a powered mechanical pump that aids the wine through the filter.

If you have a large quantity of wine to work with at the same time, then this kind of filtration is most suitable for you. You will most likely get the most exceptional filtration through this process. First assemble the system according to the instruction manual, when it's all put together, you can plug it in.

Place the tube to your system and get started. This process can produce one gallon per minute (depending on the kind of system you use, but it is speedy).

Please clean up the tools after getting the wine you need and sterilize first before using them.

Great homemade wine is not only one made with the finest ingredients but one that is appropriately filtered as well. Using any of the methods explored in this chapter, you can achieve a perfectly filtered wine that gives you a unique tasting product.

After filtering the wine, it will be ready for consumption, but first, you have to take it out of the tools and pour them in bottles.

You also have to store the wine especially if you intend ageing it a while. You will learn a lot about the bottling and storage process in the next section.

Chapter Seven

Bottling and storage

You have to place your homemade drinks in bottles and store them until you are ready to use them.

But there is a process to bottling and storage that you must learn to achieve better results.

In this section, we will discuss all aspects of bottling and the storage process that will enable round off the alcohol production process swiftly.

Bottling

We will begin with bottling. Bottling, after creating your alcoholic drink is crucial for varying reasons. Bottling is a means of storing the wine, so does it mean we can use just about any bottle? Are all bottles ideal for the bottling processes?

Well, there are no strict rules on how to use bottles for wine, but some people have specific preferences when it comes to bottling. If you know the general idea of bottling first, you can then decide based on the information you receive.

We will begin with sizes:

Bottle sizes

You can choose a bottle based on the size, colour, and how it reflects the character of the wine.

For example, most fruit wines are in long bottles, but if you prefer something different, you can experiment with the idea.

The sizes of bottles also differ as in the U.S there are bottles referred to as "Split" which are 375-millilitre bottles.

There are also the standard 1.5 litres which are 750-millilitre bottles. These bottles have a slight variation in the neck area, but they have the same kind of corks as a lid on the bottle.

There are also larger bottles that can be used to store larger batches of wine, mainly if you produce a lot and want to keep them all in one bottle.

If you make a sweet wine, then you will want to take it one sip at a time;

hence the reason split bottles are beautiful. With splits, you can achieve a single-serving process that prevents you from drinking so much with a meal.

With bigger bottles, you have fewer bottles to clean and use; hence it is an excellent bottle to consider if you want to consume your homemade wine at once. But the downside to this kind of bottle is the fact that you cannot finish the entire bottle at once and this means you will have a lot of leftover wine.

The problem with having leftover wine is that the quality tends to reduce with time, especially when you leave the bottle hanging for a long time.

Another kind of bottle you may want to consider is the 500 ml bottle which is very popular because of its decorative function. This bottle is ideal for sparkling wine and can be a great addition to your swine bottles collection.

But you should know that the higher the quality of the bottle, the more expensive it will be.

Colors of bottles

Colours of bottles are also essential, and there are generally two shades: The champagne green which is darker in colour and the leaf green one which is lighters (this has a more yellowish hue). From these two types, there are several other bottling colours, such as the brown ones that are mostly rare. There is also a clear bottle that helps showcase the colour of the content in the bottle.

A very rare kind of bottling colour is the sapphire blue which differs from the traditional green hues for bottling. This sapphire blue bottle is mostly used for marketing purposes because its fresh look lures customers as they can be beautiful. If you will have a party and you want to dazzle your guests with your homemade wine using the most beautiful bottles, then the sapphire blue is ideal.

Beyond the beauty of a bottle

Beyond the beauty of the container lies the consideration for the content itself.

What is the point in having a great looking bottle that exposes your wine to damage?

Ultraviolet rays (from the sun) causes significant damage to your wine over time.

This realization is one of the reasons why wines are in cellars to avoid filtration from the sun. So if you are going to consume your wine immediately without keeping it for a long time, you can use a clear bottle.

But if you are going to age the wine for a long time, then you might want to select a darker bottle because it will be protected from the sun.

The shape of your bottle also matters.

Bottle shapes

There are four categories of bottles, and they include:

Specialty

The champagne bottle is in his speciality category as it is a standard bottle made to handle the pressure. This bottle is thicker and very strong; it has a flair neck and is suitable for sparkling wine. If you put sparkling wine in other kinds of bottle except for this one, it will burst.

Hock

The hock bottle is slender but tall, and it is most preferred as a dessert wine. This kind of bottle comes in a variety of colours (mostly in brown and bright hues).

Burgundy

The burgundy bottle has less prominent shoulders, and it comes with a green-leaf punt. Due to its sloping shoulders, this kind of bottle will not be easy as neatly stacked as the Bordeaux.

Bordeaux

The Bordeaux is also known as the claret. This bottle has a deep punt at the bottom as this is mean to retain sediments when the wine is poured out.

The Bordeaux was crafted initially with storage in mind as it will help with stacking the bottles neatly. If you want to stack your bottles up nicely (if this is a style you acre about), then the Bordeaux bottle is ideal.

You start to bottle your wine after the creation process is complete and you have a final product. You should always scoop the wine into the bottle with care and ensure that there are no spills. Keep all bottles neatly stacked (if you are ageing the wine).

If you are not ageing it, you might want to keep it in the refrigerator but ensure that you are consuming it immediately, so it doesn't lose its authentic flavour. Always consider prices when purchasing bottles as prices are never stable, especially with the most sought after bottles.

Above all **DO NOT USE PLASTIC** bottles to store your drinks, your bottles should be made of heavy glass.

When you are ready to store the bottles, transfer the liquid from the secondary fermenter by removing unwanted sediments and minimizing air from entering the beverage as you bottle it. Fill your bottle up to 1 cm below the bottom of the cork (don't overfill the bottle).

If the bottle is excessively full, it might spill over when you lay it down in storage.

For newly filled wine bottles store them in an upright position for 2-3 days so excess air can seep out. After doing this, the bottle can be stored sideways, so the liquid makes contact with the cork.

Now the moisture from the wine will make the cork expand, and this creates a secure vacuum that seals the wine from the air.

Now we will talk about storing your wine in bottles.

Storage

You have your bottles now, and you are ready to get started with storage.

There are two significant ways you can store your wine, and they include:

Wine cabinets

Store wine in a place with the right humidity and temperature (it should be safe from vibration and light). Wine cabinets are made to enable constant temperature and also it is excellent for ageing the wine. You can easily install wine cabinets, and there are different selections.

Wine cabinets can be placed on a counter, they can be in the kitchen, and the kind of cabinet you use is dependent on the amount of wine you intend to store.

Wine cellar

If you have the resources, then you can build a cellar in your home. The basement can be as big as a garage or a small room. Cellars are worthwhile investments as they can hold more wine than the regular cabinets.

There are certain factors to consider when storing your wine at home:

The temperature of the room

Temperature is critical, especially considering how it affects the quality of the wine. To enjoy the same kind of consistent quality and flavour, you must store wines in the most suitable temperature so it can be used for a longer time.

Humidity

Humidity is an acute condition as you should ensure that it shouldn't exceed 70%. When the humidity is too high, it will make it easy for moulds to grow, thus affecting the state of the content.

No fluctuations

Some people store their wine well enough at first with the right temperature and then when variation happens, it damages the wine. The temperature in the storage should be consistent, and if you are unsure about maintaining the same kind of consistency, get a wine cellar cooling unit.

Darkness

Sunlight and light, in general, can damage your wine, so it is better to keep it in the dark. Keep wine out of direct UV rays and most of the light sources we have. Household bulbs may be safe for the content, but it can affect the labels you put on the wine.

No vibrations

Store your wine in a place without vibrations which is why the basement or a separate room is always best as vibrations and continuously moving the wine will speed up the chemical reaction in the wine and spoil it.

Wines should be kept separately

Keep all bottles of wine away from areas that are exposed to strong odors.

Place wines on the side

It is best to lay bottles of wine on their sides so the corks will stay moist and stop air from getting into the liquid.

With this chapter, you now know how to bottle and store your wine which is a very crucial part of the process. If you create a masterpiece of wine using the recipes in section two and you don't store the wine well enough, you will miss the entire purpose of creating the wine in the first place.

There are common challenges that happen when distilling at home. Some people try to distil for the first time, face these challenges, and they give up. But if they knew what to do to avert those issues, they would enjoy the process, next, you will learn more about these problems and how to solve them.

Chapter Eight

The most common problems and solutions with distilling at home

The hallmark of all acquired knowledge is to know the impact of both

sides of an idea. When you learn something beneficial, it is also imperative that you know its pros and cons, so you have a balanced narrative. In creating your distinct blend of homemade alcohol, you may encounter some challenges and issues.

Some people give up on the entire process because they weren't prepared for such challenges, so they didn't know how to handle them.

I want you to be 100% ready for the process as such; it is the reason we have to take pre-emptive measures now.

Problems may occur at varying stages with the product, but if you know about such issues beforehand, you can avoid them. The information in this chapter will also help you make adequate preparation for the process itself.

Now don't worry about reading only problems, as for every issue you read through below you will find solutions.

Let' get started!

Unsuitable environment

Some spaces are not ideal for distilling alcohol at home. If your space is filthy then you shouldn't begin the process there, if it is too cold or hot, you might want to reconsider. More so, everything you need to make the process happen should be within your grasp so you can seamlessly move from one step to another.

The right environment will cause you to enjoy the process, and this will make it easier for you to look forward to creating more alcoholic beverages in the future.

Unsterilized equipment

The importance of cleanliness all through this process is paramount as most of the issues people have while distilling at home are attributed to germs that come from unsterilized tools.

Don't sterilize your instruments the very moment when you intend making a new batch of alcohol.

Sterilize them a few hours before you get started and ensure that after using the tools, they are washed and kept clean for later use. Even if you've got the most fantastic recipe for your wine, if the equipment is unsterilized, you will have issues.

Adding too much sugar to your mix

When producing alcohol, the yeast needs sugar as this is the essence of the fermentation process (the yeast consuming sugar and turning it to alcohol).

This realization means that the amount of sugar in the yeast will ultimately control the amount of alcohol that will be made. If the sugar level is too high, it will serve a preservative function and negatively impact the fermentation.

The solution lies within knowing how much sugar to add based on your choice of fruit and the other ingredients you will use in making your alcohol.

For example, if you are using California grapes, you wouldn't need added sugar, and you will still get about 10-13% of alcohol.

You can also control your sugar levels using a wine hydrometer that tells you how much sugar you have inside the mix and how much should be added.

Old yeast

Always ask yourself how long you've had the yeast and for how long have you been using it before adding it to your mix. Yeats is a living organism with a minimal life span. Which is why when you buy yeast, it is placed in a pack, and it gains its life back when putting in water.

The problem starts when your yeast is stored in a room with a temperature of above 80 degrees. If you save the yeast in a freezer, it will also lead to severe issues as well. Always know the duration of your yeast and save it well enough for you to use it effectively anytime.

Failure to throw out the heads and tails

When your still starts to produce, you MUST get rid of the heads, which is the first 50 ml out of the stills. When we get to section two, you will gain further clarification on what this means, but the point is that there are harmful substances in those parts of the alcohol.

You don't want to take harmful substances with your alcohol now, do you? So it is important that you throw out the heads and even the tails for a better-tasting and healthier drink.

Icy fermentation conditions

A significant condition you will find in all the recipes you will find in part two is the right temperature when fermenting. If the room is cold or extremely hot, it can affect the mixture. You cannot afford to pay less attention to temperature because it determines a lot of things. The yeast you intend to use will become dormant when the temperature is below 60 degrees. If the yeast was re-hydrated in warm water (about 105 degrees) and placed in a cooler environment, the yeast can experience thermal shock and cause it to become inactive.

Always observe the temperature while distilling hence the reason you will need a thermometer. If the temperature isn't right things can go wrong.

Nothing happened after adding yeast long ago

Your mixture is supposed to react to the presence of yeast, so if after two or more days nothing happens, then there is a problem, it means your mixture isn't fermenting. This situation could be because of a bad seal used between the lid and bucket. Fermentation will take place, but the CO_2 that should be released is still trapped. Fix your cap and ensure that all equipment works well.

The yeast may also not be working because of bad yeast. If your yeast is not good enough, it will become inactive.

The liquor smells like vinegar

There are several reasons why your drink may smell like vinegar. A significant reason is the presence of bacteria. Aceto bacteria and Lacto bacteria are prevalent contaminates, and their impact on the drink can lead to it smelling vinegar.

Now in some cases, people like the vinegar smell because it has a different taste. But if you find this smell worrisome then maybe you should be more meticulous with sanitation such that there is no chance of bacteria getting into your mixture.

Beer that wouldn't stop bubbling

Some people complain of homemade wine that bubbles excessively well if your beer bubbles for more than three weeks it may still be okay. The bubbles may be because the fermentation was too cold and the yeast worked slower than it was supposed to.

This situation may only pose a problem if you don't like the bubbles, which means you have to monitor the temperature during fermentation to be sure that you are on the right track.

Using unripe fruits

Your final product may have an unpleasant taste or look dull because you used unripe fruits (for recipes where fruits are needed). A piece of excellent advice you should hold on to when creating your liquor is to use fruits when they are in season. If you have to use grapes, then ensure that the grapes are ripe and ready for use.

Some wines also do not last long because of the inclusion of unripe or overly ripe fruits. You must get the perfect match for your wines fruits are base ingredients which means that if you don't get right at that level, there will be problems with the wine.

It is always safe to know the problems you might encounter and get rid of them even before they happen. This chapter has presented insight into some of the challenges you may face as you distil at home. But we also read through solutions which means that for every problem you have answers.

Some of the issues highlighted above happen in an unplanned way, so don't be so hard on yourself. There are times when even when you get everything right, you might still make some minor mistakes. Learn from the mistakes, understand why it happened and make necessary corrections.

Distillation at home is a continuous process and one in which you get better every day as you use the skill. You will eventually get better with time such that you no longer make such minor mistakes.

Do you have some questions about the process? Are you curious about additional information?

Then head over to the next chapter to get answers through the FAQ

section.

Chapter Nine

Frequently asked questions

This last chapter of this first section will be on some frequently asked questions (FAQs) that home distillers ask to gain clarity of the process.

Questions are essential because they help shed more light on aspects of creating a unique alcoholic beverage. The answers to the questions will help you make the right decisions and also cause you to understand why certain things happen while creating your homemade wine.

Now when you get to part two of this book (the practical section), you will unravel a wide array of recipes for different beverages. This realization is the reason why the questions and answers you will find below, will cut across different types of alcoholic drinks and aspects of our discourse thus far,

This is an opportunity for you to get answers to some of the questions you may have. This chapter will prepare you for the practical section in part two, so get ready to unravel insightful information.

How can I ascertain the strength of my homemade alcohol?

You can do this with the help of an alcometer which is a device with a scale on it that measures alcoholic content. If there is a higher concentration of alcohol, the density of the liquid will be lighter, and the alcometer will sink to the bottom. Then you can read the scale to know the amount of alcohol present, and this will also help you dilute the mixture correctly.

Can I use aluminium still instead of copper still (would it affect the end product?)

Some people use aluminium stills, but you should know that it can become very messy. With aluminium stills, a lot of cleaning is required, and your alcohol will have a metallic smell that may be unpleasant. So if you can stick with the copper still.

How long does it take before I can ferment the wine?

The duration varies based on certain factors such as the kind of yeast you use, the amount of sugar in the wine and even the temperature. While some wine takes up to two or four weeks to ferment, others may take additional time.

What is the best kind of thermometer to use for distillation at home?

To check the temperature inside the still, you can use any kind of thermometer that can go from 100-300 degrees. But when preparing the mash (which is the base of almost all types of alcoholic beverage), you will need a standard thermometer meant solely for pulps. The mash thermometer should be within the range of 32-150 degrees.

What's the quantity of alcohol to be thrown away from the batches I make?

Due to the risk of methanol in the liquid, you must pay close attention to the quantity you should throw out, and this is usually the liquid that comes first. Always throw away the first 50 ml with every production.

Where can I buy the tools and equipment I need to distil at home?

You can get all you need at online stores such as eBay and Amazon. You can also make purchases from stores in your environment.

Can I dilute the wine I make with water?

Of course, you can dilute the wine with water. But this is based on individual preferences, taste the wine first and decide if you want to dilute it or not.

Can I use any kind of yeast for this process?

Different kinds of yeasts offer varying flavours, but brewers yeast is the best option because it gives the alcoholic beverage a better taste than regular yeast. Always ask questions at your local brewery or supply stores to understand the various kinds of yeast (if you seek other alternatives).

What are the critical things that affect the quality of my final product?

Your choice of stills

You can use a pot still which collects the condensate from boiling and condenses it. You can also use a reflex still which has a different chamber that purifies the condensate before condensing it. Regardless of your choice of still if you follow the directions carefully, you will get a great product.

Alcohol percentage

The last result you get on the rate of alcohol is also an essential factor in determining the quality of the product.

The type of wash

To get the best quality, you must use very high-quality yeast that helps maintain the right temperature for fermentation. If you distil unwanted spirit and do it excessively, you will end up with a poorly created product. Your wash should also contain the best of other ingredients needed to make the right product.

Storing and the ageing process

Storing your product in a cool dark place will help produce a burst of flavours with your drink. While some home-distillers use oak barrels to store their products, some others also add oak chips to the spirit, and this can give a fantastic finished product.

The kind of carbon treatment

Always stick to a reputable brand for carbon that is made specifically for creating such a product.

How many litres of homemade alcohol can I store in my home?

Well, it depends on the alcohol laws in your local community or country. For example, in the USA, you cannot have non-taxed liquor in your home, and the same rule applies to some Western-European countries as well.

In some countries like Britain and the Netherlands, you can produce only a specific quantity of alcohol, and you will be breaking the law if you exceed the amount. With this question, I will advise that you understand the law concerning alcohol creation in your country and abide by it.

What if my homemade wine has a bad smell or taste? What did I do wrong?

Well, the wine could have an offensive sulphur smell (mostly like that of rotten eggs) for varying reasons. The first reason is that your production kit may be unsuitable for the process. The second reason could be that you used too much of a particular ingredient which affects the product. The third reason could be because the batch is contaminated (this happens when equipment is not adequately sterilized) when bacteria sets in, it affects the fermentation process.

Can whisky be diluted with ice?

Yes, you can dilute your homemade whisky with ice. When the ice melts the ABV reduces, and this reduces the high concentration in the liquid.

Is it safe to make my spirits? Is it legal?

Distilling alcohol at home is not allowed in some countries. In countries such as Austria, New Zealand, Russia, Romania, Ukraine etc. it is legal to distil a home. But in some other countries, there might be an outright ban on production or a restriction on the amount to be produced. If you are caught producing alcohol at home when it is illegal in your country, you will be breaking the law. In some countries and cities, you will need to get a license first.

Yes, you can use scraps of wine as you will solely be taking out the alcohol. Even if the wine is dusty, the distilled product will still be useful.

Where can I get an airlock?

Airlocks are easy to get in stores and online as well. More so, you can make one for yourself as it is a prevalent household item.

Can I create moonshine without an ageing process?

A lot of people leave the spirit as it is after creating it without allowing it age. It depends on your personal taste; you may want to age because you want a peculiar taste, and you may not want to as well (work with what you prefer).

Is it natural to make my alcoholic beverage?

It is natural to make your alcoholic beverage at home. In time past (hundreds of years ago, people made their spirits without government regulations). So it is reasonable to desire such a homemade product, but we live in a different time now where there are laws for such things so you must be careful.

Why is my homemade brandy colourless and the one I bought at the store has colour?

The reason for the difference in colour is ageing. Brandy that ages in wooden barrels or with additions such as honeycombs and wood spirals affect the flavours. These additions also have an impact on the colour. If you didn't age your brandy, the colour would still be bright, unlike those in the store made by professionals who age for a long time.

The questions above were arranged in no particular order, and I hope the answers you read helped you understand the process even more.

With this section, we have come to the end of part one (the theoretical aspect of our journey). It is time for you to apply all you've just read in section two by taking a more practical approach towards the learning experience.

Get your aprons ready as you are about to create the most amazing alcoholic beverages in your home.

This second part is the fun section of our experience together because this is where you start to put everything you've learned from part one into practice.

There are multiple kinds of alcoholic beverages you can create at home, but it wouldn't be possible to present all of them.

So we will concentrate on six primary forms of alcoholic beverages.

But here are a few things to remember before we start as this is a practical step you will implement at home:

Always check local laws regarding distilling before you go ahead with the process.

Avoid distilling around open flames as the alcohol vapour can cause an explosion

Keep your distilling space neat and tidy at all times (we don't want germs in our drinks now, do we?)

Don't pressure yourself to get it perfect the first time. You will get it right for sure if you don't the first time be excited about trying again

This section will be all about steps, so pay close attention to each step so you can minimize or avoid making mistakes.

Try to get all ingredients needed before the day you chose to distill

All practices below are merely for home use and not for industrial purposes.

Lastly, enjoy the process!

Chapter Ten

How to create home-made whiskey

We will begin our practical section with a common alcoholic beverage that is incredibly tasty: whisky.

While the whisky you buy at the store is excellent, preparing your unique blend allows you to create a signature drink with the kind of ingredients you desire.

Through this process, you will learn how to make a whisky brand that suits your taste perfectly.

To get gallons (which is 7.6 litres of whisky), you will need:

- ❖ A clean pillowcase/clean cheesecloth
- ❖ I cup champagne yeast (please check the manufacturer's instructions before using this).
- ❖ A burlap sack (large)
- ❖ Water (5 gallons which are also 19 litres) you might need more warm water when you get to the sprouting stage. Follow the instructions carefully, and you will know when.
- ❖ Whole untreated kernel corn (10 pounds, .5 kg)

We will begin making whisky now.

Step one

The first step entails sprouting the corn and making the base of your whisky, which is the mash. To sprout the kernel corn you have to get it wet and allow the sprouts to grow. After the corn is sprouted, it is ready to be made into a mash. This mash is a combination of grains and warm water, the enzymes inside the mash will break down the starch in the gain, thus producing sugar.

Step two

Put 4.5 kg of untreated kernel corn into a burlap sack and put the sack in a bigger bucket or container. Saturate the burlap sack with water (please use warm water) please make sure the corn soaks evenly as this is crucial for the end product.

Now you may be wondering "Why should I sprout the corn for the whiskey".

Well, you sprout the corn because it eliminates the need for sugar that could have been added to the mash. Without added sugar, you will have a delicious and organic whisky made with the finest ingredients. Sprouting (also referred to as malting) enables enzymes in the corn to convert starch to sugar (the sugar then becomes the foundation of the alcohol in the whisky).

Step three

Allow the kernel corn to sprout for 8-10 days by keeping the bag in the dark, warm space (a basement is an ideal space). Ensure that the corn remains is damp for about seven days and while sprouting keep the corn's temperature between 62 and 86 degrees.

Step four

Now remove the sprouted ends of the corn when it is ¼ inches long/ rinse the corn in clean water and remove the grown roots by hand while discarding the sprouts.

Step five

With a rolling pin, wooden muddler or any other equipment, crush the kernels in the fermenter until they have all been broken apart.

In some cases you can use a grist mill to crack the kernel open, just make sure it dries up properly so it can go through the grist mill.

Step six

Pour 5 gallons of boiling water on the corn mash because at this stage you are ready to ferment.

Step seven

Now you will ferment the mash, but first, you should know that when making whiskey, all instruments and tools MUST be kept clean.

If you work with unclean tools in a polluted environment, the whiskey itself can become contaminated. Contamination can ruin the entire whisky so you must sterilize thermometers, airlocks, containers (and their lids) as well as your hands (do this before you start).

Step eight

Let the mash cool down to about 86 degrees (always use a thermometer to test the temperature). What you want to achieve here is a fresh mash that is also still warm enough for the yeast.

Step nine

Next, put the yeast on the top of the mash, close the lid on the fermenter and leave it for about 4-5 minutes. Then pitch the fermenter to one angle while moving it back and forth (this will agitate the yeast and cause it to start working).

Step ten

An airlock is crucial for fermentation as it allows CO_2 to escape without air getting to the mash. I air gets into the mash, the effect of the yeast will be affected, and it will ruin the entire process. You can also make an airlock if you don't want to buy one (but it is not an expensive item, so it is advised that you buy one).

Step eleven

The process of fermentation will take 5-10 days (this depends on the temperature, yeast and the amount of grain you use). With the help of a hydrometer, you can confirm when primary fermentation is complete. If the thermometer gives the same reading for more than two days, then distillation can begin.

Remember to keep the mash at a steady level (77 degrees), and while fermenting, you will need heat or the yeast to become active (this will make it consume the starch). After fermentation of the mash strain and siphon it into a still.

To strain the mash, use a clean pillowcase or cheesecloth to keep solids away from the still when transferring the mash.

Now you are ready for distillation.

Distillation process Step one

The mash that is free from all solids is referred to as either a wash, sour mash or wort. The wash should have about 15% alcohol in volume and distilling it will increase the alcohol content. To achieve better results, get a pot still.

Step two

Heat the wash slowly until it gets to a boil but remember not to rush the whisky distillation process. Heat the still (medium heat) for 30 minutes to one hour until it boils. If you heat the wash-up too quickly, it will lead to lead to a burnt wort with burnt flavours. The temperature at this time should be at 172 degrees to 212 degrees.

This temperature is ideal because alcohol and water have varying evaporation levels. While alcohol evaporates at 172 degrees, water evaporates at 212 degrees. This realization means that if you heat up the wash to 172 degrees band not beyond 212 degrees, the evaporated liquid (inside the still) will be alcohol and not water.

Step three

The condensing tube is meant to take the evaporated alcohol and cool it off quickly, but you have to turn on the tube when the wash is at 120-140 degrees. Gradually, the condensing tube will start to bring forth liquid.

Step four

Throw out the heads. The head is a mix of inconsumable compounds that evaporate into the wash. The compounds include methanol (this is a poisonous compound). The heads usually come out first so for an 18-litre gallon throw away the first 50-100 ml.

Step five

After the heads are gotten out, you will be ready to get the right part. When the thermometer on the condensing tube gets to 175-185 degrees, you can start collecting the valuable part, which is the body of the distillate.

Step six

Remember to throw out the tails which comes out when the thermometer reads 205 degrees. Turn the heat off, so the pot cools down. So what you have now is a high ABV (Alcohol by volume) whisky which may be too harsh for you to drink. For you to get whisky that is close to what you have in stores, you have to dilute it to about 40-50% ABV.

Step Seven

Before you dilute you will want to know the ABV level first and to do this, you can use proof and tralle hydrometer. The readings of the proof and tralle can be confusing so try not to get confused. The poof will be twice the amount of tralle (this is how you get an accurate reading).

Step eight

Now you are ready to age the whisky!

The whisky can go into the barrel when it is at 58-70% ABV, this process makes the whisky smoother and gives it a very rich taste, but the whisky must age in barrels and not in bottles, if you put it in a bottle it will stop ageing.

Oak barrels are also the best options; they can be charred or toasted barrels. You can get the barrels from other distillers that have aged whisky in them before. You can ass some toasted oak chips into the barrel, the chips are aromatic and will give the whisky a unique taste.

If you use the oak chips option, you should strain the whisky to remove the chips before consumption after removal put the whisky back in the barrel and allow it steep between 5-15 days (or longer based on your personal preference).

Step nine

Next, you have to dilute the aged whisky before you can bottle or drink it. At this stage, the whisky is about 40-45% ABV which guarantees better taste.

Step ten

Now you can bottle your whisky and drink responsibly!

Whisky is always a great tasting alcoholic beverage, but to get the distinctive rich taste, you must follow the instructions and processes carefully.

The final product you get will be worth the entire process, and you will be glad you took on this adventure.

Let's learn how to prepare brandy in the next chapter!

Chapter Eleven

How to make Brandy

What is better than homemade brandy? Nothing!

Most people who create their homemade brandy at home attest to the fact that it is the perfect alcoholic beverage for summertime as brandy is always bursting with flavours and a fantastic aroma. Here you will learn how to create your brandy at home using fruits; you will find comprehensive and easily applicable steps below.

Before going on, you should know that in selecting your choice of fruits, you have to settle for options that are great for a brandy product.

For example, grapes are not an ideal choice for homemade brandy because the grape distillate is considered too harsh and to reduce its harshness, you will have to age it in an oak barrel.

You can use other fruits such as apples, pears and plums for your brandy base.

First, you will need:

- Your choice of fruit Glass jar
- Potato masher
- A container (made of either glass or ceramic. Not metal or wood).
- Yeast Bottles Still
- A large pot Towel
- A measuring cup Heat source

Let's make brandy now!

Step one

Start by selecting the fruit you want.

When you make brandy, you preserve the flavours of summer fruits that are processed into a bottle of wine.

Now you have two choices here:

You can make your wine by gathering fruits and starting the fermentation process for a month before you can distil your brandy.

You can start distilling brandy using purchased litres of fruit wine. After deciding on the type of fruit wine, you want to use, move over to the next stage.

Step two

Ensure that the fruit you chose are in season so you can get the ripest bunch that is fresh and ready for use. You will need about 3 quarts of fruits which can yield enough wine for a considerable batch of brandy. You can harvest and ferment more fruits if you want to make more brandy.

Most of the commercial brandy brands you've seen are made out of crushed grape skins. The grape distillate is harsh hence the reason it must be aged in an oak barrel to get that harshness off. But because you are making brandy at home, I will advise that you stick to other fruits and not grapes. Other fruits will also give you the same great- tasting brandy without the more extended ageing period that is required with grapes.

Step three

Now you can process the fruit by first washing it thoroughly and cutting it into slices. Don't peel the fruit but ensure you remove the pits.

Step four

Mash the fruits in a jar (glass or stone crock jar). Use a potato masher or any other convenient instrument to mash the fruits as this will help the fermentation process. At the bottom of the jar, add a layer of fruit, add sugar and continue this process until the fruit and sugar are completely used.

If you are still going to use berries (berries are lower in sugar than most fruits) which means you wouldn't need added sugar. The stone crock should be large enough to take up all fruits with a few inches to spare as this is because the mixture will bubble up during fermentation.

If you cannot get a stone cock, then use a glass bowl or any other thick container.

Step five

Add the yeast and water by dissolving six teaspoons of dry yeast in a cup of water (please use active dry yeast and not instant yeast bought at stores). Put the yeast mixture over the fruit and sugar mix then add six cups of water (cold water).

Step six

The liquid inside the crock will begin to bubble as fermentation starts so you will need to get all overflows. Also, leave the mixture in a cool and dry place for seven days.

Step seven

Don't leave it untouched in the seven days as you are supposed to uncover the crock and with a long clean spoon stir the content. Then cover it again as the alcoholic content will increase daily. Then you will have to leave it for an additional four weeks.

Step eight

Now you can bottle the wine at the end of the four weeks. Pour the wine into glass bottles and cover-up adequately. Store the wine for some months so you can achieve a deep flavour.

Step nine

Get a still that is small enough to be placed on a stove. You can use a 1/2 – 2 litre of alembic copper still, which will be just right for this purpose.

You can get good stills in places where kitchen wares are sold or online. You can also use the still you buy to make other beverages discussed thus far in this book and for different mixtures.

If you get a new still or a used one ensure it is clean before use. First, you can experiment with a small batch of brandy as this will help get the flavour into the still. More so, starting with a small batch will help you get the process right before moving on to larger quantities.

If you enjoy the small batch process, you can make more brandy by upgrading to 5 gallons (now you will need an 18.9 litre still).

Step ten

Now with your base wine and still you will also need clean glasses, spoon and other things to make the distillation process possible. Ensure that your workspace is clean before you begin. You will need a Dutch oven with a large pot that is big enough to take in the still.

The pot will be filled with water, and then you can use it as a boiler to take control of the heating process for the still. Also, get glass containers because when the still starts producing, you will need the containers to retain what comes out of the pipes. A sealable large glass jar will also be helpful in storing the brandy when it is ready.

Step eleven

Fill the Dutch oven with some water and place the still inside. Add more water (if necessary) the water should rise above three quarters to the sides of the still. Place the Dutch oven and the still on the gas burner (or any other heat source).

If you are using the 5 gallons (18. Litre still) then you should know it wouldn't fit into the Dutch oven so you can skip this step and place it directly on the heat source.

Step twelve

You can now fill the still (3/4) with wine. Regardless of the size of still you use, always leave the top at least ¼ empty, so when the wine heats up, it can increase.

Step thirteen

Put the lid on the still and connect the tube from the lib to the condenser coil. Put cold water inside the condenser and place a glass under the spout so you can collect the alcohol it produces.

Varying still products come with their peculiar instructions so please do not assume based on the general guidelines for still usage. Read the instructions carefully and use the still's directions. By following the instructions, your brandy will be well processed.

It is time to distil!

Distilling the wine

Step one

When you are making brandy does not allow the content in the still become too hot. The wine has to get to right simmer level, but it shouldn't boil. Start by heating the still using a high flame and keep it elevated until it is strong, but it shouldn't boil.

If you notice that the alcohol drips too quickly on the sides, then you have to turn down the heat as the alcohol shouldn't drip for more than one drop per second.

You will also know that the alcohol will flow soon when you touch the copper tube as when it is hot, the alcohol will soon start flowing. Remember that the slower the liquid flows out, the better your brandy will become.

As usual, get the foreshots (which is about 7.5 ml per 1.5 litres of wine), if it has a powerful, sharp chemical smell then throw it out as it isn't consumable. Also, get rid of the heads which are not pleasant, but if you want to make another batch of brandy, you may want to keep the heads as it can be useful when it is distilled a second time. Continue to smell the distillate as it flows out and then gets rid of what isn't needed until you get to the hearts.

You will know you have the hearts when the smell gives you that aroma of fruits you used in making the wine (it smells divine).

You will smell this aroma without the harsh smell of acetone, more so the distillate should not be milky, and it should be clear. Collect them in small glasses while monitoring carefully for any change in smell or texture.

Make sure also to adjust the temperature when necessary (this should be as the distillation process comes to an end). Increase the heat to get the same flow level and continue to turn it up until you get one drop every 1-3 seconds.

However, do not overheat the still and do not allow it to boil.

The last part of the distillate is the tails which are less concentrated and also less tasty.

At this stage, you will even notice a change in the smell as the fruitiness will no longer be present. Discard this milky looking tails and turn off your heat.

At this point, you will have about 300 ml of brandy which means you can store it in a jar (use a tight lid).

Now don't worry if you smell your brandy and it has a strong acetone smell, just place a small piece of cloth on the top and allow it breathe for while overtime the lousy smell will dissipate.

Then you can age the brandy!

Do not hurry and start drinking because the ageing step is essential. Screw the lid on and store the brandy in a cool place for a few weeks (or several months depending on what you want to achieve). When you open the bottle after the ageing process, you will find a smooth tasting brandy than the first one you distilled, which is your final product.

Well done, you have followed through with this process till the end. Your dedication is a testament of your commitment to the process.

We will continue on our journey with the next chapter on how you can create moonshine!

Chapter Twelve

Creating moonshine

Moonshine is a popular alcoholic beverage consumed by millions of people, a significant reason why it is so popular is because of the unique blends that go into the production process as you will discover in this chapter.

Remember to enjoy all alcoholic beverages responsibly to avoid alcoholic abuse.

Most of the time to create your alcoholic beverage at home, you will need to start with the base, which is always the mash. Some people who struggle with distillation at home make mistakes with this step hence the reason for their struggle.

If you get it right with the process of creating your moonshine mash, you will get the rest of the process right so always pay close attention to the beginning details.

There are different kinds of pulp for moonshine; some purists believe that corn whiskey mash is the best option for a richly-flavoured paste.

This belief in the value of corn has made some corn farmers distil their corns to create excellent tasting moonshine for profit. Aside from the corn approach, you can also use the "Sugar shine" approach (which is very popular for beginners).

This sugar shine approach eliminates the corn flavour and creates a unique moonshine taste.

One of the most striking details about moonshine is the fact that you can use a wide array of ingredients to create the final product. This versatility with components has led to the availability of varying moonshine products based on individual preference.

An interesting approach is the "Hybrid approach" that supports the corn mash with sugar. The added sugar can double your mash production as it is much more convenient while enabling the individual to achieve traditional flavours.

Although for this book, we will use the conventional corn whiskey approach, you should know that you have the creative freedom to create your unique mash blend.

Your creativity can be based on your choice of ingredients (you can always do this much later when you have gotten better with creating the traditional moonshine).

So how do we create moonshine?

Let's find out!

We will begin with the corn mash recipe, and you will need:

- ❖ Fermentation bucket A long spoon
- ❖ Mash pot
- ❖ Gallons of water (5) Yeast
- ❖ Malted barley (crushed, 1.5 pounds) Heat source
- ❖ Thermometer
- ❖ Corn maize (flaked, 8.5 pounds)

The process Step one

Put the mash pot on your heat source and add the 5 gallons of

water. The water should heat up to 165 degrees.

Step Two

Turn off the heat source when it gets to 165 degrees and stir in the

8.5 pounds of flaked corn maize. Continue stirring for some minutes within 30 seconds interval until the temperature gets to 152 degrees.

Step Three

After the mixtures cool off add the 1.5 pounds of crushed malted barley. Then check to ensure that the temperature is stable (check every 30 seconds).

Step Four

When the mixture cools to 70 degrees, add yeast but please note that it will take some hours before the temperature gets to 70 degrees. You can speed up the process by using an immersion cooler.

Step Five

Ensure to aerate the mixture by placing it in and out of two containers for about 5 minutes. Add the mixture to your fermentation bucket as you are now ready for the fermentation process.

Fermentation

To ferment the mixture, you will need:

- Citric acid Siphon
- pH meter (this should be an advanced meter) hydrometer
- cheesecloth

Leave the mash to ferment for about 1-2 weeks (room temperature). The right temperature is critical here because if the room is too cold, it can affect the fermentation process. After all, the yeast will become inactive.

To achieve good results with temperature, you should use a hydrometer to confirm the start of the fermentation process and when it is complete (just to make sure all sugars are used). Which means you have to write down the gravity reading when fermentation begins and then the reading at the end of fermentation.

The formula will also help you ascertain the amount of alcohol that will be produced.

Next, you have to strain:

The straining process

To strain, all you have to do is siphon the mash water from the mixture. Ensure that you leave all solid materials in a container (this aids the adjustment of pH).

Strain the mash water using a cheesecloth.

At the advanced distilling level, you may add about two tablespoons of gypsum to the mash. Then test the pH of the water because the ideal pH is 8 to 6.0 which means if the pH level is too high you can use citric acid to bring it down and calcium carbonate to increase it.

Well done, you are doing well thus far so let's get on with distillation, shall we? To distil you will need:

Column packing Moonshine still Cleaning products

The fermented and strained mash water

To become a good moonshine distiller, you must practice, which is why I recommend that you take notes through this process.

Note how everything turns out and what works so the next time you can do better with the process.

First, you have to prep your still for the process by first ensuring it is clean (I know I have repeated this all through this practical section, but it is because it is most important). To avoid a salt build-up that will affect the final product, you must clean your still.

If there is packing to your column, then you should pack it with the right amount of copper that is appropriate for the set-up process. If the setup has a condenser, then ensure to hook the water input and output.

Now you can add your mash water to the still. Use a cheesecloth or an auto-siphon if you've got one) to transfer the mash water to the still (remember to avoid the inclusion of solid materials). You need to try to reduce all sediments in the water to 0%. Next, you have to run your still (which is the fun part of the moonshining process).

Running your still is also known as the distillation process, and it entails separating the different chemicals by using different evaporation temperatures.

During this process, you are not creating alcohol s you are only separating it from other substances present in the mash water.

During the fermentation process, you had already created all the alcohol with the help of the yeast.

Next, bring your temperature to 150 degrees and when you get to this level if you have a condenser turn on the condensing water. Get your heat source to a high level until the still starts to produce. Check the timing for your drips until you achieve 3-5 drips every second.

When you get to this level, reduce the heat to maintain a medium setting.

At the distillate, level ensures that the drips are getting into a glass container and not a plastic one.

If you use plastic, the product will be laced with BPA, and this will cause several other issues for your health.

Remember to get rid of the foreshots, heads and leave the hearts. You can use the tails later for another distillation process.

With this process, you have succeeded in creating the right moonshine product. Allow the set-up to dry and cool off in a dry place.

With moonshine, in particular, you are working as a scientist that pays specific attention to the process. For some people, they learn how to create moonshine the first time and cannot re-create the same great tasting product because they didn't pay attention to their process.

It is possible to get better with your moonshine production and become an expert, but it is also possible to fail at it the second time. To get better at it, you must keep notes of previous trials and be inspired to experiment with a wide array of ingredients. Sometimes you will love the final product when you try new components and sometimes you wouldn't like it; it is all okay. So long you keep trying, you will surely get better.

Moving on now from moonshine, we will learn how to make rum in the next chapter.

If you have always been a fan of rum, you will enjoy the processes encapsulated in the next section, more so you will learn how to make different types of rum.

Chapter Thirteen

How to make rum

Unlike other spirits, rum has a much simpler production process, yet the procedures for making rum at home differs from person to person. However, in this chapter, you will learn how to create rum, and you will also read through details on some of the different methods for making rum in a range of flavours.

Due to the different ways of producing rum that cut across varying cultures, there are different ingredients you can use, but all of them are from one primary source: sugarcane plant. Rum is made with unsulfured molasses, which is a product one gets from refined sugarcane.

The reason you should use unsulfured molasses is that sulphured molasses contains sulphur oxide (this serves as a preservative).

The process of sulphuring gives the molasses a chemically-infused flavour, and this isn't right for your rum hence the reason for unsulphured molasses.

You can also use raw sugar cane or its juices if you don't have access to molasses.

In this chapter, we will use both molasses and the natural sugar cane, so the rum has a sweet caramel and vanilla flavour, delicious! A lot of rum recipes use unsulphured molasses gotten from sugarcane plants. The molasses flavours are in light, blackstrap, and dark (you can get blackstrap molasses for the rum wash).

Making rum, the wash recipe

- Heat source Thermometer Brew pot
- Raw sugar cane (8 pounds)
- Blackstrap molasses (1 gallon) Long spoon
- Rum turbo yeast (the one for professional use) Water (6.5 gallons)

The sugar/molasses wash process

Step one

Put your brew pot on the heat source and pour in the 5.5-gallon water.

Step two

Heat the water to 125 degrees and stir in the raw sugar cane and molasses. Stir the mix with a long spoon until it is all dissolved (please note that you may have to stir for a long time until he molasses disappears entirely).

Step three

After the molasses and sugar are dissolved, add 1 gallon of cold water, so the temperature is not too high.

Step four

Check the temperature of the wash regularly (stir at least every 30 seconds of 5 minutes). When the temperature gets to 80 degrees (after several hours but you can speed up the process if you are using an immersion cooler).

Step five

After the wash cools to 80 degrees, add the rum turbo yeast and aerate the wort. You can aerate the wash by placing it in and out of two separate containers for at least 5 minutes).

Step six

Pour the wash in the fermentation bucket, place the cap and airlock it by sealing the fermentation bucket with an airlock. Store in a dark place (at 75 degrees to 80 degrees).

The process of fermenting the rum wash

You will need:
- Cheesecloth Citric acid
- Advanced pH meter

The fermentation process for rum that includes molasses is different from the one made with raw sugar cane.

The wash made from fresh sugar cane ferments for 3-7 days, and when it is ready, it will have a sweet taste. The sweet taste is because of the yeast's ability to convert the sugars in the wash. Fermentation is complete when gas doesn't come out of the airlock in the bucket kit.

The process of straining

After fermentation is complete, you have to remove all solid materials, and cheesecloth is ideal for straining. At the advanced level, some distillers test the pH of the wash; first, the pH should be 4.5 to 5.0, and citric can bring it down if it is too high.

Now you are ready to distil your rum. You will need:

- ❖ A still burner
- ❖ Fermented and strained rum wash Cleaning products
- ❖ Easy-to-use siphon Hydrometer
- ❖ A pot still

You are doing great at this moment as you have done all that's necessary to produce your fermented rum wash.

The rum wash you have now contains unwanted content that should be separated and disposed of, and this is where distillation takes place.

Distillation makes the rum wash purer and concentrated; the process also separates unwanted materials such as acetone, methanol, and acetaldehyde.

First, you must clean your pot still (please do not skip this step as it will determine the quality of your finished product).

Next, add your rum wash into the still (use a siphon for this step)

Make sure the still is well set up, then turn up the heat source and raise the temperature of your rum wash through two distillations.

At the first stage, you will collect all the distillate (without separating anything, you will separate at the second round of distillation).

If you are working with a condenser, then turn on the water when the boiler gets to 130 degrees.

At 168 degrees, the still will begin its production so you can increase the temperature to continue the production of distillate.

When it measures less than 20%, ABV, stop collecting distillate (you will know this with the help of a hydrometer).

Hold on to the content in the still because you will add it back to the second distillation. This process will contribute immensely to the great flavour of the rum.

With 20% of water dilute the first distillate, stir it well and place it back in the still. Now begin your second stage of distillation.

The next step entails collecting the rum distillate, and it is similar to the way you obtain the distillate of other products. First, discard the foreshots (the first 5%).

Then discard the next 30% (heads) until you get a sweet-smelling aroma. Next, you have to age the rum.

Aging

Aging the rum can be done in different ways, and it is influenced by a variety of factors, as explained below:

The type of barrel

A major factor to consider is the type of barrel; you have to know if it should be a charred barrel or a new one. If you work with a charred barrel, the rum will have a dark and rich flavour, with a new barrel, it will have a lighter taste.

The time the rum is aged

Duration if another crucial factor as the longer you age the rum, the more it will take in more of the flavour of the kind of barrel you use.

The area of production

The area in which you produce the rum also matters; if you create in the tropical climate, the rum will mature faster, and this will be because of the amount of product that is lost to evaporation. Before you start the aging process always distillate to 50%.

As mentioned earlier, you can create several types of rum such as white rum, dark rum, and spiced rum, let's find out how you can get such variations.

Spiced rum

When you are done aging the rum, you can add more flavouring such as spices, vanilla, cinnamon, cloves, nutmeg, etc. at this stage; you can experiment with spices and flavours and get to know what you like more. First, mix the spices in another container and not in the rum barrel.

You have to be certain of the spice you want to use before adding it to the barrel.

Dark rum

In some countries, rum is aged for distillation for at least a year while this isn't required at all times; if you want dark and rich flavoured rum, you will have to age it for about 6 -18 months. The aging process for this type of rum has to be in an oak barrel with oak chips that give it a unique flavour.

Regardless of the duration, you chose to age the rum ensure that the blend is consistent when mixing as this is the last step for a good and adequately aged before bottling.

White rum

For the white rum, it is usually very light as such aging is not required; all you to do is dilute the drink with water. When it gets to 45%, you can blend the mix, bottle the spirit, and leave the bottle untouched for about four days.

Within the four day duration, the flavour will stabilize, and this means your rum will age without a dark colour.

Now your rum is ready, and you can create different variants from this process using the information in this chapter. Next, you will learn how to make vodka from the comfort of your home.

Chapter Fourteen

How to make vodka

Vodka is one of the most loved alcoholic beverages, especially by people who like drinking neutral spirits.

Vodka doesn't age, and it is made from fermented fruits, sugars, potatoes, and grains, to produce alcohol. As a homebrewer, you have to be very cautious with the vodka distilling process as you must discard methanol, which can be damaging when consumed.

The fact that you will be distilling at home with minimal or no supervision means you should be extra careful with the entire process.

Pay close attention to the steps you will find below and ensure that you keep your distilling space clean at all times.

Preliminary steps and general information

First, you will have to choose your ingredients (the ones you want to ferment into vodka).

Vodka is commonly made from rye, corn, potatoes, barley, or wheat. You can also use sugar and molasses, which can be added ingredients or used as a stand-alone ingredient.

Regardless of what you chose, they must be sugars or starches because this is what produces alcohol.

When you add yeasts with sugar or starch, it births alcohol and carbon dioxide.

If you are making vodka from grains and potatoes, you must create a mash that will contain active enzymes that break down the starch from grains into fermentable sugars. If you are using fruits, then you wouldn't need the paste as fruit juice already contains sugar after fermentation. Wine can be a medium that is distilled into the vodka.

You may have to add enzymes based on what you decide to make your vodka from; the enzymes will change the starch to sugar. If you settle for grains and potatoes, you will need more enzymes as these are high sources of starch; as such, they will need enzymes to break down the starch into sugar.

If you chose malted whole grains, then you will not need additional enzymes. Malted barley and wheat are rich in enzymes that break down the starches into fermentable sugars. If you work with refined sugars, then you don't need additional enzymes because sugar is already available. You can settle for any of the mashes, but for this book, we will focus on potato mash recipe for your vodka.

First, you will need the following:

Ingredients for the base

- ❖ Gallons of water (7)
- ❖ Thermometer
- ❖ Mash pot
- ❖ Long spoon
- ❖ 25 pounds of potato
- ❖ Crushed malted barley (5 pounds)
- ❖ Heat source

❖ The mashing procedure

Start by scrubbing the potatoes with a produce brush (this removes all dirt)

Cut the potatoes into cubes to increase the surface area

Boil the potatoes for 20 minutes in 7 gallons of water

Mash potatoes using an immersion blender or by hand

Transfer the mash to the mash pot. Add water to reach a total of 7 gallons in volume

Increase the heat of your paste to 140 degrees, stir the mix continuously until you get the desired temperature.

Add five pounds of crushed malted barley and stir continuously while adding barley.

Hold the mash at 140 degrees for about 20 minutes and stir for 30 seconds every 4 minutes.

Increase the temperature to 152 degrees and hold it for 1 hour while stirring for 30 seconds every 10 minutes.

Read the gravity level if it is below 1.065, add sugar to reach

.065.

Cool the mash to 75 degrees, and if time allows you to cool, you can do so overnight. When kept overnight, the enzymes in the barley have time to break down the potato starch.

Fermenting the potato vodka mash

For this next stage, you will need:

- ❖ Yeast
- ❖ Siphon
- ❖ Citric acid
- ❖ Fermentation bucket
- ❖ Cheesecloth
- ❖ Advanced ph Meter
- ❖ Iodine (this is optional)

Fermentation process

Start by creating a yeast using the steps below:

Sanitize a mason jar

Pour sanitized water into the jar (it should be 4 oz of 110degree)

Add two teaspoons of sugar to the water and stir

Mix the yeast in (the amount depends on the type of yeast you use, always follow the directions).

Stir the mixture

Allow the starter to sit for 20 minutes; you will see the volume of the mixture double.

Transfer the mash liquid to the fermentation bucket. Pour the mash through a strainer to do this and try to aerate the mixture by making a splash, but don't lose liquids.

Add the yeast starter to the fermentation bucket and add an airlock.

Ferment the mixture for two weeks at room temperature.

Use iodine to check if the fermentation is complete by taking a sample of the liquid off the top.

Place the sample on a white plate or a lid and add a few drops of iodine. Watch the sample closely; if it turns blue, then it means it has reacted completely to the starch. If starch is still present, then it implies fermentation is not complete, so you will have to check again in a few days.

After fermentation is complete, you will have to remove solid materials as if they are leftovers; they can cause headaches. You can remove such solid materials with cheesecloth as this should be done before distillation.

Now we are ready for distillation!

The process of distillation

Below are the tools you will need for distilling vodka

Still

Cleaning products

Mash water (fermented and strained)

Column packing

At this point, you have completed the most significant part of the vodka making process, but it is not perfect vodka yet.

You have to separate the vodka from other unwanted stuff, and this is the distilling process.

First, you must prepare your still as if you want a great tasting vodka you must ensure that the still is very clean. Next, add some neat copper packing to your column; if you are working with a condenser, hook up the water and then add your wash to the still. You should use an auto-siphon for this process so you can reduce the amount of sediment.

Next, you have to run your still, so ensure that the column is packed with copper packing. Turn up the heat source and increase the temperature of your wash. If you are working with copper still, apply some flour paste to the joint between the vapor one and column when it reaches 110 degrees. If you are using a condenser, ensure that the water is turned on when the boiler reaches 130 degrees.

At 170 degrees, the still will begin production, and you will want to dial in your heat source to get 1-3 drips every second. The next step will be the collection of your potato vodka distillate.

The most exciting part of this entire process is collecting your vodka. However, this is where you have to pay even closer attention.

You have to know what to throw out and what to retain, so here is the breakdown:

Throw out the foreshots

The first 5% of the run will be the foreshots that contain methanol (it is volatile and toxic), so please do NOT consume this part of your mix.

If you consume methanol, you can develop some health issues of which blindness is a possibility.

Isolate the foreshots and throw them out.

Get rid of the heads

The next 30% of the vodka is the heads; it is similar to foreshots and also contains volatile alcoholic substances. A significant part of the heads is known as acetone, which has a distinct smell. Although acetone will not make you blind if consumed, it will give you a most terrible hangover. Isolate the heads and throw them out.

Keep the hearts

The next 30% is the hearts, and it is a sweet part of the vodka. The solvent smell of acetone will wear out, and you will perceive the sweet smell of ethanol.

At this point, you know you have succeeded with distilling your vodka, but you will need your sense of smell to be on high alert as to know when to smell the hearts, identify the heads, and see when the foreshots are out.

The tails

The last 35% will be the tails; it contains protein and carbohydrates from the wash you don't need in your product. Ethanol concentration decreases with the tails so you can set the tails aside and use them as wash later.

Congratulations are in order as you have just learned how to make delicious potato vodka.

Don't worry if you have a little variation with your first attempt as with time and consistent repetition; you will get it right.

Also, don't forget to clean up after getting your vodka, wash everything you used, and maintain a neat distilling space.

What is the next alcoholic beverage on our menu?

It's beer!

Flip over to the next chapter to learn all about mixing things up to create tasty bottles of beer.

Chapter Fifteen

Mixing up for a beer

Beer is a trendy alcoholic beverage, as regardless of where you are in the world, you will surely find a unique type of beer consumed by the locals.

With a few ingredients and some materials, you can brew beer at home in mini-batches.

If you enjoy the process of creating beer, you can do it repeatedly until it becomes a full-time hobby.

Here is a list of ingredients and materials you will need for beer processing:

- ❖ Kitchen thermometer

- ❖ Bottling container (get an empty container, clean water bottle or a food-grade plastic bucket)

- ❖ A filter (the type that strains grains)

- ❖ A brew pot

- Bottles for your beer

- Clear poly-vinyl tubing (3 feet of 3/8" (this will aid siphoning and fermentation)

- Rolling pin (aids with crushing the grain)

- Large funnel

- A container of bottled water (3 gallons) will provide water for the beer, and also it can be a container used for the fermentation process.

- 3/8 cup of sugar (suitable for bottling)

- 3 lbs light dried malt extract

- 1 oz brewer pellet hops (Northern)

- One pkg brewer's yeast

- 8 oz crystal malt (crushed)

With these ingredients and materials, you are ready to get started! Please note that there could be variants of beer that can be made at home.

This recipe is just one of many and will introduce you to the idea, as you do I regularly you can devise new processes and mixtures.

Step One

The first step is to crush the grains. Place the 8 ounces of crystal malt in a large freezer bag. With a rolling pin, crush the grains and try not to make it very smooth. You are not supposed to get a flour-like texture, just a coarse texture, as the aim is to break the grains. When you decide to take this beer-making process seriously, you can purchase malt mill from stores that are designed specifically for this process.

Step Two

Steeping is referred to as the brewing term for the extraction of all the goodness in the grains. Pour ½ gallons of water from your 3-gallon water bottle and mark the 2 ½ water level.

Then pour 2 ½ of the remaining water into your brew pot (make sure you leave at least 3 inches to the top). Then add the grains you crushed and turn on the heat to medium-high while bringing the temperature to 150 or 155 degrees.

Turn off the heat, cover the brew pot, and let the process commence inside the pot (leave it like this for 30 minutes). With a strainer, remove the spent grain (don't worry if you still have some in the pot).

Step Three

The content of the brew pot should boil, and afterward, it should be removed from the heat as you stir in the malt extract. Put it back on the heat to boil, but at this stage, you must pay close attention to the pot so you can avoid overcooking the content. If you have a boil-over, you will have to clean up the sticky mess, and it isn't a pleasant experience.

After controlling the boil, add 2/3 oz of the hop pellets to the boiling pot and leave it to boil for 60 minutes (this will help you get the best out of the bittering nature of the hops). Place your filter in the boiling pot so it is sanitized for about 15 minutes (you will use it later).

Turn off the heat after 60 minutes and add the rest of the hop pellets. Cover the pot, let the new hops steep for 10 minutes as they will add to the flavour and aroma of your beer.

Step Four

Now you can work on the airlock. You can use a commercial airlock or create one from clear vinyl tubing with one end to the cap and the other in a cup of water. Commercial airlocks can be bought at stores for $1 (including a starter kit).

But if you don't want to use commercial airlocks, you can drill a hole of about 3/8" in the water bottle cap. The airlock will fit the hole, and the whole idea of this process is to allow the carbon dioxide produced during fermentation escape without air from outside, getting inside.

Step Five

Now at this stage, you have wort. Wort is "Unfermented beer," and it has to be cooled. An excellent method for cooling is to have a cold bath in the sink to submerse the brew pot (not entirely). Add some ice to the bath as it will help to accelerate the cooling process, then swirl the pot in the cold liquid.

When all sides of the pot appear cool (when you can touch it), you know it is ready for the next stage. But first, at this point, sanitation is essential because the beer is almost available for consumption.

Whatever comes in contact with the wort must be sanitized, or else you will make the mixture develop critters that multiply in the wort giving your beer an undesirable flavour. Sanitize everything you use with the wort, such as your funnel, by soaking them in a solution of 1 tablespoon of bleach for 30 minutes.

Step Six

Start pouring the cooled wort through the sanitized strainer and funnel into the fermentation bottle. The total volume of the fermenter should be 2 ½ gallons, but your brew pot was huge and made it easier for you to boil ½ gallon you will have to compensate for the evaporation that happened while it was cooking.

If you need to add more water from the gallon, then you can use tap water or water from the ½ gallon you poured off previously.

Step Seven

Now you are ready to pitch the yeast. Pitching the yeast is a brewing term for the addition of yeast to the unfermented wort. If the wort (the one in your fermenter) is at room temperature, then you can pitch your yeast. You will know if it is at room temperature when the sides are warm enough to touch. If the sides are not warm enough, then you should allow it to cool down before pitching the yeast.

Please note that most of the time, a package of brewer's yeast contains enough yeast for a 5-gallon batch. Don't pour the entire content into the fermenter, use about half of the pack, you can add a little bit more, but it shouldn't be lesser than the required amount.

Step Eight

Now you will have to leave the yeast to work over 7 to 10 days as it converts sugars in the wort to alcohol and carbon dioxide. Put the fermenter in a cool and dark place, it doesn't have to be a very dark place, but this is also a crucial part of the process. Do not place it under direct sunlight.

The process of fermentation is always enjoyable to observe; however, you shouldn't worry if nothing happens within 12 to 24 hours as, after this time, you will see foaming and bubbles that escape from the airlock. After the 7 to 10 day period, the fermented sugars will complete its conversion through the yeast.

Step Nine

Now you have your beer!

But we are not completely done at this point. If you drink the beer, now the taste will be flat; as such, you must complete the process through priming. Priming entails adding a measured amount of additional fermented sugars before bottling commences. The active yeast in your beer will convert the added sugars to carbon dioxide in the bottle.

The carbon dioxide will not escape the bottle, thus leading o the creation of carbonated water. Then boil 3/8 of sugar (which is ¼ cup and two tablespoons) you might want to use corn sugar or table sugar all in one cup of water for 5 minutes. Cover the mixture, allow it cool down and pour into a sanitized container that can hold your beer (this can be another large water bottle or empty plastic bucket).

Take the beer from the fermenter into the bottling container (please be careful while doing this) Now your beer is primed! What should you do next?

Bottling!

Step Ten

When you start brewing beer at home, remember to get beer bottles for the final stage of the process. You will also need caps or a keg that will contain your finished product. There are several options for the first time you brew, so feel free to experiment as soon enough you will stick to a particular bottling choice.

You can also purchase empty bottles and caps, or get reusable bottles and caps. Champagne bottles are great alternatives as well; what matters the most is that the bottles are sanitized before usage. You can soak the bottles in diluted bleach for 30 minutes and rinse with clean water.

Step Eleven

The next step is known as aging, and it entails keeping the beers in bottles for at least seven days, so the fermentation takes place inside the bottle. This process will also carbonate the beer, just ensure that the beer is placed in a cool dark place for a minimum of 7 days and a maximum of 10 days. Do not open the bottle too early, and don't put it in the fridge yet.

During this time, the beer will start to become more transparent because the suspended yeast will settle at the bottom of the bottle.

Step Twelve

Drink your beer!

After the ten days, you can place the beer in the fridge, so it's chilled. Open the bottle and pour yourself a glass. The beer will taste excellently well, and you will have developed a tasty brew.

When beer tastes that good, the fun can begin with friends and family at home, which is one of the critical objectives of this book: to empower you with information that will help you do things the right way the first time.

In the next and last section, you will find details on how to create distilled wine from home.

Chapter Sixteen

How to create distilled wine

The last section for us on this journey is a detailed chapter on how to distil wine at home.

Wine is one of the most loved alcoholic beverage in the world, a lot of people love wine for varying reasons, and it is only natural for anyone who loves wine to learn how to distil at home.

This section will be a fun last chapter, so get your aprons ready, and let's dive in!

First, you will need the following materials:

- ❖ Dutch oven

- ❖ Dish soap

- ❖ Water

- ❖ Towel

- ❖ Sponge

- ❖ Copper still

- ❖ Wine

- ❖ Glass jars (clean ones)

- ❖ Glass containers

Step One

Get a copper alembic pot that is mostly used by beginners and professionals alike. The pots are available in a variety of sizes, but I will advise that you use the 1-liter pot, which is equivalent to 0.26 US Gal. you can also use the 2-liter size, which is 0.53 US Gal as they are also manageable when used for distilling purposes at home.

These alembic pots can be purchased online, and if you haven't done this before, you might also want to consider a teakettle. A teakettle will serve as an experimental tool to distil small batches of wine first before making more significant purchases.

Step Two

Put the still in a pot, and this pot has to be large enough to contain both still and water. The Dutch ovens are high for this because they can hold up to two litres of still.

Step Three

Now fill the pot up to a three-quarter level with the water, you can pour tap water into the Dutch oven but don't make it excessively full. If it is too full, it will overflow and ruin the entire process.

Step Four

Next, pour the wine into the still (not the Dutch oven). It should be three-quarters full of wine and try not to fill it beyond this because you must be mindful of bubbles that will show up at the top when the still is heated.

Please note that for your choice of wine, you can use store-bought wine, and the amount you will require is based on the still you will use.

After getting better at distilling, you can try this process out with homemade wine instead of store-bought.

Step Five

The next step entails running a tube from the pot o the condenser by first placing the lid on the still. The condenser comes out of the lid's top, and it has a spout that can be attached to the copper tube. Place the end of the tube in the spout in a separate bucket (don't worry as all of these parts are included with the still when you make a still purchase, you will see these other parts).

While some condensers have different spouts, the one facing downwards is attached to a tap. Attach the second tube to the upward spout and set the other end in your sink. If you discover that you don't have these parts, you can create your condenser coil using a copper tube and bucket.

Step Six

Next, you will add cold water to the condenser. Fill the bucket (not the still) with cold water so it can chill the evaporated wine into a liquid. At this point, the condenser tube should be inside the bucket with the spout on the side. So long the tube is stuck on the spout, the bucket will not leak water.

If the whole set up doesn't fit well on the still, combine ½ cups of rye flour with three tablespoons of water and place the mixture on the loose area. As the still receives heat, it will create a seal.

Step Seven

Place a glass under the spout, also have lots of glasses close by because you will have to rotate them to get the distillation as it drips. The first glass can be a larger jar or bottle as the first millilitres you get wouldn't taste right, so that you will discard it.

Step Eight

Now you are ready to heat up the wine. The first thing to do is to turn the heat high until the alcohol drips. Make sure you keep a close eye on the still because if the water gets too hot, it will boil, and this will make the distillation drip into the glass even faster.

If the drip is too fast, it means you will get less alcohol in each drip. You can always adjust the drip speed to your preferred level as you practice distilling.

Also, do not use an open flame as an electric burner indoors is a safe option. You can also use a propane or natural gas burner (outdoors).

Step Nine

Now you have to lower the heat so distillation can continue, so the water temperature should be at 78 degrees (you can place a thermostat inside the condenser's spout). Always watch the drip speed to keep track of the temperature, and when the distillate drips (one or three times every second), it is a sign that you're still is at the right temperature.

Step Ten

Check your distillate and change the bottles, but for you to do this, you must frequently check to see how the wine is doing. To avoid spills, replace the bottles, and this will improve the quality of the wine as it drips. Also, have a taste at this point to ensure you are on track with the process.

Step Eleven

The foul-smelling distillate should be thrown out, and this is often the first 50 millilitre (it is undrinkable). This early 50 millilitre has lots of acetone and wood alcohol; it is poisonous and has a rancid smell. This liquid is also known as the foreshot, and it isn't right.

Step Twelve

After the foreshot drains out, you will get the drinkable alcohol next. You can tell it is drinkable because of its fruity smell (it will smell like the fruits/herbs used in the wine).

Now the still is even hotter and may drip at a faster level, so collect the small liquid glasses and switch them as they fill up. You will most likely get 2 litres of quality wine (could be less but around this number).

Step Thirteen

The distillate will start to look milky, throw it out when it loses its colour. Also, smell it and detect the aroma, when the odour is out, the wine is mixed with water and undrinkable alcohol, throw it out.

Cleaning

Now that your wine is ready, you have to clean up afterward.

Remember that what you are distilling will be consumed as such the process for creation and post-distilling matters in ensuring proper hygiene.

Start by turning off the heat by providing the burner is turned off. Then give the still some time to get cold and move the wine to a cool cellar or cabinet.

Remove the still and be careful with dropping it so it doesn't break, and you can use it another time.

Remove the still's condenser and lid, pull the cover off and wash the still with soap and water. You can also clean the copper pots with salt and vinegar because it mostly starts to look green after use.

Now you can chill at your favourite corner in your home with your perfectly distilled wine.

With this practical chapter on wine distillation, we have come to the end of an exciting and enlightening journey.

The next section is the last and concluding one that contains a call to action, prompting you to take execution seriously.

Conclusion

Well done, you have shown exceptional commitment to the learning process, and I believe you are equipped with the necessary information to get started.

Now what we have achieved together is so important because we live in a world that is powered by increasing access to knowledge and information.

In this modern world, no one has any excuse not to know anything or how to do things the DIY way.

The only thing stopping you from creating a distinct product is your access to knowledge. Once you've got the expertise and USE it, you can create whatever you want.

Now the emphasis on the previous statement was the word "Use." What is the point in having access to knowledge you don't intend using, and why should a person take the time to learn something without using it?

So at this concluding section, I want to remind you of the power of execution.

This book was intentionally split into two parts for easy assimilation of knowledge. But the split was also to show you how to use the information you've gained.

First, you had to read through the section on foundational concepts; then, you moved on to the practical aspect because it is not enough to know the basic ideas.

Could we have rounded off the entire experience with the first part?

Yes, we could, but I wanted you to have a more robust learning experience hence the reason for part 2.

Even as you put this book down, remember that no one cares about what you know; no one will be impressed when you say,

"I can distil wine at home."

They would be impressed when they take a sip of your product because execution is all that matters.

Your first attempt at creating your unique distilled drink may not be perfect, but you've got to keep at it. The more you try, the better it gets, and this makes you even more experienced with the process.

Remember to have fun with it, share your experience with other people, and be creative with your home-made process.

Cheers to the good life enriched with the most satisfying alcoholic beverages you create from the comfort of home.

Best wishes!

www.ingramcontent.com/pod-product-compliance
Lightning Source LLC
Chambersburg PA
CBHW071623080526
44588CB00010B/1243